# A SPACE FOR UNKNOWING

*To Samuel and Charles*
*with thanks just for being*

Stephen R. White

# A Space for Unknowing

THE PLACE OF *AGNOSIS* IN FAITH

the columba press

First published in 2006 by
the columba press
55A Spruce Avenue, Stillorgan Industrial Park,
Blackrock, Co Dublin

Cover by Bill Bolger
Origination by The Columba Press
Printed in Ireland by Betaprint, Dublin

ISBN 978 1 85607 544 2

## Table of Contents

# Introduction

One of the curious things about writing theology – or, I suppose, any other kind of writing as well – is the strange variety of different ways in which successive books come to be written. Sometimes a central idea will come, apparently from nowhere and almost demand to be explored and fleshed out; on other occasions a train of thought may be sparked off by someone else's work; or one might wish to examine further an idea which one has touched on previously in one's own thinking. This last possibility is very much the case with this present book: it is at once a new beginning and a gathering up of unfinished business from a previous essay in theology.

Thus my thinking here springs from some ideas developed at least briefly in the course of writing *A Space for Belief*. These are the two related ideas first, of theology as creating that 'space for belief' rather than being primarily a system of rigid propositional definitions of faith, and secondly of there being a constant need for provisionality in all of our thinking about God, and a need to acknowledge the limits of such thought, realising always that God is ultimately beyond anything that we are capable of thinking or formulating about him.

At this point a very brief clarification of terms might be useful. Thus in the title of this book I have referred to the concept of 'unknowing', and in the sub-title I have used the more technical term 'agnosis'. These terms are, for all practical purposes, synonymous, the only difference between them being, I would suggest, that the term agnosis carries with it a more varied cargo of theological associations, rather as a heard musical note carries with it its own unheard – yet vitally present – harmonies. As a convenient shorthand for all of this, I propose to use the less

familiar term agnosis throughout the course of this study, but if
this intrusion of a technical theological term should cause any
reader to balk, he or she should feel entirely free to substitute the
word 'unknowing' whenever the concept of agnosis hoves into
view. Having explained here the meaning of this central term,
agnosis, it is worth pointing out that apart from this word I have
kept technical theological terms to a minimum. Inevitably, however, some have crept in, and I have therefore included a short
glossary of these terms at the end of the book.

Whether one prefers agnosis or unknowing, however, the
theological impact is much the same, and with this agnosis or
unknowing in mind, it is the case that as John Polkinghorne so
picturesquely describes it, 'The Infinite will never be caught in
nets spread out by finite minds',[1] and therefore Christian theology is always to be done in a creative tension between gnosis
and agnosis, such that whilst it may reasonably claim to be intellectually defensible it can never claim to be intellectually prov-
able. As with so many facets of theology, this creative tension is
perfectly delineated by Richard Hooker in his celebrated *Lawes
of Ecclesiastical Polity*, in which he comments:

> Dangerous it were for the feeble braine of man to wade farre
> into the doings of the Most High, whome although to know
> be life, and joy to make mention of his name: yet our sound-
> est knowledge is to know that we know him not as in deed he
> is, neither can know him: and our safest eloquence concern-
> ing him is our silence, when we confesse without confession
> that his glory is inexplicable, his greatness above our capaci-
> tie and reach.[2]

This position, and these ideas, whilst they were sketched out
and thereafter alluded to in a variety of contexts in *A Space for
Belief*, seem to me, however, to merit a substantially fuller treatment in and of themselves than was possible within the confines
of that discussion. This is so principally for two reasons. First,
these two concepts of a space for belief and a consequent provisionality are ones which reach to the very heart of any theologi-

cal endeavour and address its fundamental concerns – indeed the very presuppositions and conceptual assumptions on which that endeavour and any framework built upon it may rest: What can we know? How can we know it? And even more importantly, in what sense and with what degree of confidence can we base our lives upon this 'knowledge'?

One's reaction to these questions will, I am well aware, depend upon the mind-set with which one approaches them. To some they will appear as deeply threatening questions and there may well be those who throw this book on the fire having read no further than this. To others, however, the mere fact of asking questions such as these is the medium of life, hope and excitement both in theology and more broadly in the life of faith as a whole.

For the asking of these questions (in the light of our twin concepts) suggests that they are open questions and will remain open if we bring even a measure of agnosis to our questioning, and this is a large part of the never-ending fascination, indeed the thrill, of the theological task rightly understood. It is a thrill which George Pattison clearly shares when he remarks: 'Precisely because the height, length, depth and breadth of God remain as yet unthought, there is occasion for the undertaking I call "thinking about God".'[3] And in a sense, the even greater frisson attached to the whole undertaking is that the questions will still remain open even after other thoughts have been brought to expression, including the present ones. The task of any theology, once it finds the necessary humility – and, as we shall argue, the courage – to grant a substantial place to agnosis, is not to 'pin down' God or indeed any aspect of faith's relationship to the divine, but rather simply to attempt to polish one odd facet of the ever-emerging jewel of faith and to prompt, inspire or challenge us to see something of that jewel and of him with whose reflected light it shines a shade more clearly. And so, in a sense, the primary purpose of this exploration, or of any work of theology, is to stimulate others – whether through the pleasure of agreement or the irritation of disagreement – to seek yet more

urgently, and to refine and polish still more. Whatever the result, the issue is one which concerns the nature and task of theology, and this surely, at least, matters.

Thus the second reason why finding a space for belief and
living with provisionality deserve a deeper exploration here is
that our answers to the questions which we have posed above
and our response to the claim for the necessity of provisionality
will underpin our whole approach to theology thereafter and
will influence both how we understand God and also therefore
how we understand ourselves and our response to him; for this
understanding and response will clearly look very different depending upon our primary response to the issues we have
raised. A theology which abhors agnosis and provisionality will,
self-evidently, be very different from one which welcomes them,
and this will in turn have ramifications not merely for how we
set about theology, but also for how we approach specific areas
of Christian life such as ecclesiology and even ethics. The whole
shape of theology, the church and our Christian life may well
hinge upon our response, positive or negative, to the concept of
agnosis as a theological *fundamentum*.

This book, then, is very much a personal exploration of these
various themes, and it is therefore quite deliberately not written
in a heavily referenced academic style. In part this is simply to
avoid the danger – all too common in more overtly scholarly
works – of becoming so bogged down by minutiae that the reader
(and often apparently the writer) loses the thread of the argument. More importantly, though, it is to allow the thoughts
which follow to be 'my thoughts'; to be, however inadequate, at
least fresh and original – something which is needed in every
generation if theology is to remain vibrant and stimulating.
Indeed, Kierkegaard reminds us in *Fear and Trembling* that this
new thinking in every generation is an absolute given requirement for theology: it is not only desirable, it is inevitable:

> Whatever the one generation may learn from the other, that
> which is genuinely human no generation learns from the
> foregoing. In this respect every generation begins primitively,

has no different task from that of every previous generation, nor does it get further, except in so far as the preceding generation shirked its task and deluded itself. This authentically human factor is passion.

But the highest passion in a man is faith, and here no generation begins at any other point than did the preceding generation, every generation begins all over again, the subsequent generation gets no further than the foregoing – in so far as this remained faithful to its task and did not leave it in the lurch ... (each) generation has in fact the task to perform and has nothing to do with the consideration that the foregoing generation had the same task.[4]

If for Kierkegaard this re-doing of the theological task is simply inevitable and unavoidable, then, by contrast, for George Pattison it is something to be welcomed with open arms, and is a way of doing theology for which he makes a particularly eloquent and impassioned plea:

Theology is a discipline with an extraordinarily long and tangled history, and it is consequently very easy for theologians to become commentators upon commentaries upon commentaries – and so on ad infinitum. That thinking about God requires engagement with the tradition and with its contemporary context is not something I wish to deny. However, it is all too easy for the contemporary theologian to defer the moment when it is necessary to stop and think, to ponder seriously the nature and direction of one's own thinking and to consider why one is committed to this particular way and what its consequences are. As we add our voice to the surging polyphony of the historical development of ideas, it is important that it really is our own voice.[5]

Others will decide whether that voice most closely resembles a theological equivalent of Dietrich Fischer-Dieskau or Florence Foster Jenkins, but either way it is at least the personal voice of one who has attempted to 'stop and think'.

Finally, since as we have noted already, there are many

Christians who become deeply worried and start to man the theological barricades whenever uncertainty in the realm of faith is mentioned, it is important to stress that agnosis – the realisation and acceptance of our condition of unknowing – is not new in Christianity. It is indeed as old not merely as Christianity but as the religious quest itself. Far from being a new idea it is one which has always been interwoven with our Christian faith and its roots in Judaism, both in the long history of each of these faiths and indeed in scripture. It is, rather, that today the concept is an unpopular and neglected one which is sorely in need of rediscovery and rehabilitation if our faith is to be as rewarding and exciting as it has the potential to be.

In the light of this, this study falls into two parts. In the first three chapters we shall examine the roots of agnosis in scripture and in the Christian tradition and seek to establish afresh that far from being a new and destructive religious category, agnosis is not only thoroughly religiously 'respectable' but also life-enhancing. This theme of the importance and the enriching consequences of agnosis for our faith will then be taken up in the remaining chapters as we explore the reasons why a measure of agnosis is especially necessary today and how it might offer a new vision and new vitality to a faithful but all too often somewhat gray and downhearted church.

First, though, the 'very beginning' as Maria quickly realised, is 'a very good place to start', and so we may usefully turn, at the outset of our search, to the Old Testament and to the Jewish experience of agnosis as a consistent part of their response to God.

# CHAPTER 1

## *Old Testament Agnosis*

Agnosis is probably not the first concept which springs to mind when we think of the Jewish understanding of faith and experience of God in the Old Testament, but this is equally probably because 'unknowing' is not what we are looking for as we read the text. We are, understandably, attracted to or fascinated by other and more overt aspects of the many vivid and colourful Old Testament stories, and we are therefore prone to miss the quieter but consistent thread of agnosis which runs through it all. As one reads these stories one might indeed be forgiven not only for missing the note of agnosis, but for detecting what appears to be an overdose of certainty. God's commands are transmitted in detail to the Israelites through Moses; the prophets are certain that they speak God's message to his people – and are astonishingly harsh on those who preach a false message; the Israelites are certain of the command to kill every living thing as they conquer the cities of the promised land, and so on.

To acknowledge this is simply to pay tribute to the Old Testament authors' flair for compelling storytelling; and yet alongside this sense of divinely ordained certainty there runs another voice, quieter perhaps and prone occasionally to get submerged under a torrent of events, yet always present as a questioning counter-melody to the headlong rush of the dominant theme. There is an awareness of the ultimate mystery of God, a faltering of the footsteps as one approaches things divine, and a recognition that there is always more of God than we have yet discovered, and indeed more than finite minds will ever grasp. There is, in short, an undercurrent of agnosis which surfaces from time to time in a variety of forms, and whose pres-

ence, far from being overlooked, should form a vital and rewarding part of our reading of the Old Testament.

Of the various characters and stories which evince this tendency towards agnosis, there are at least three which are, in different ways, particularly revealing. These are the characters of
Job, Jonah and 'The Preacher' of Ecclesiastes, each of which offers a subtly and distinctively shaded version of the theme.

Of the three, the most immediately arresting and complex
presentation is that contained in the book of Job. This is largely
because of the intricate patterning which is created, especially
towards the end of the book, between the neatly packaged but
platitudinous and illusory 'certainties' of false knowledge, and
the altogether more disturbing but profounder truth of agnosis.
The matter comes to a head for Job in chapter twenty-eight and
again in chapter forty-two. Throughout the book Job's three
friends, Eliphaz the Temanite, Bildad the Shuhite and Zophar
the Naamathite – joined later on by Elihu – have been attempting to account for God's actions towards Job and to explain to
Job the ways of God. Job, in turn, has been less than persuaded
by their arguments, and in chapter twenty-eight he (rightly)
questions the possibility of there being any full human understanding of God or his actions, and in so doing he reveals the
shallowness of his interlocutors' arguments. Job asks in verse
twelve of this chapter: 'But where can wisdom be found? Where
does understanding dwell?' and answers himself in the following verse: 'Man does not comprehend its worth; it cannot be
found in the land of the living.' For Job, wisdom and understanding reside in God alone, as he makes plain a few verses
later in his discourse:

> Where then does wisdom come from?
> Where does understanding dwell?
> It is hidden from the eyes of every living thing,
> concealed even from the birds of the air.
> Destruction and Death say,
> 'Only a rumour of it has reached our ears.'
> God understands the way to it

and he alone knows where it dwells,
for he views the ends of the earth
and sees everything under the heavens. (28: 20-24)

This much is reasonably straightforward, but the end of Job is
notoriously resistant to satisfactory interpretation. It does not
constitute the whole picture or provide a magical hermeneutical
key, but the concept of agnosis certainly provides some degree
of illumination when we try to fathom the final chapter of the
book. Two things in particular appear to be happening. First,
and most straightforwardly, Job's friends are chastised by God
for their folly because they have not spoken of God 'what is
right': their apparent certainties and neat solutions are finally
proved to be, as Job had rightly divined, illusory. Secondly,
however, and initially perplexingly there is a further realisation
taking place on Job's part, following the revelation of God's immensity and majesty in God's speech which extends from chapter thirty-eight to the end of chapter forty-one. It is perplexing
because in his speeches Job appears to have been 'on the right
lines' and he is commended by God for speaking what is 'right'
of God. If this is so, then what is the purpose of God's lengthy
speech in which he appears to be haranguing Job for his limitations both of might and of understanding? The answer – or at
least an answer – would seem to be revealed in Job's speech
which opens chapter forty-two. In the course of this short speech
Job says: 'Surely I spoke of things I did not understand, things
too wonderful for me to know' (42:3). Perhaps what this speech
reveals – and what God's monologue was designed to reveal – is
that Job's previous concessions to agnosis had not gone far
enough. Certainly he had seen through the spurious 'knowledge' of his friends, but he had met this with too much assurance on his own part. He may have spoken what was 'right'
about God, but what he now needs to realise, and in this speech
does realise, is that even this 'rightness' takes in only a fraction
of the reality of God (it is 'right' as far as it goes, as we would
say), and that there is a mystery and immensity about God
which is still, and will forever be, outside his ken. In the ac-

knowledgement of this human limitation in the face of divinity Job's story ends, and ends significantly in blessing as he becomes richer and surrounded by a larger family than ever before. Perhaps there is even some correlation between our ability to receive blessings and an acknowledgement of our inability to explain them?

Alongside Job, the story of Jonah appears to be simplicity itself, but here too the author explores at some depth, through the medium of his deceptively simple – indeed almost naïve – tale, the nature of religious agnosis. Significantly, Jonah illustrates rather than grasps for himself the substance of agnosis, and there is thus a deft and ironic sting in the tail as far as the reader is concerned. Jonah is firmly locked into the pre-conceptions of his own understanding of God. These lead him some way towards a knowledge of God's nature and likely activity, such that he tells God that the reason why he had tried to flee to Tarshish was that he knew that God was 'gracious and compassionate' and 'slow to anger and abounding in love' (4:2), and that God would not therefore destroy the people of Nineveh once they had repented and changed their ways. What Jonah does not see, either now or through the following episode of the vine and the worm, is why God is concerned in this way for a foreign people. He does not grasp that to be 'gracious and compassionate' is not simply a choice which God makes, but is of the essence of God and is therefore the primary purpose and desire of God in his dealings with people. Jonah knows that God will forgive a repenting people, but he seems to think that God's preference (like his own) should be for the people not to repent and so to deserve destruction: what his vision cannot encompass is that God's will is actively for repentance and salvation even for the worst of sinners. Jonah is angry at the people of Ninevah's repentance and cannot comprehend God's concern and compassion for them which rejoices in that repentance. It is significant that the book of Jonah ends with a question-mark, and we may well doubt whether the (admittedly mythical) figure of Jonah ever understands the events of which he has been a part, or grasps more fully the nature of the God behind them.

There is, admittedly, nothing in all of this of conscious agnosis on Jonah's part. Jonah, one cannot help feeling, is simply blind: he does not know that he does not know! Yet we mentioned that there was a sting in the tail for the reader, and it is in this that the subtlety and distinctive genius of the book consists. Here is a short, delightfully simple tale about someone who, whether through wilfulness or ignorance, cannot see things which we, the readers, can see all along. The more Jonah cannot see, the wiser we, by contrast, come to feel, until … until we make a vital connection and realise that our own lives may look to others just like Jonah's life looks to us! Unknowing and limits of under-standing (especially about God) are inherent and inescapable parts of being human, and the sooner we realise that and dis-cover the depth of inadequacy in our own understanding and knowledge of God, the better!

The situation is different again with Ecclesiastes, and there is another, and perhaps even more thought-provoking facet of irony at work. As with the book of Job, Ecclesiastes represents something of a *nemesis* when one comes to interpret it rather than simply revel in the timeless beauty of its poetry, and there-fore one is acutely aware that what follows may turn out to be, in the words of 'the Preacher' himself, nothing more than 'vanity'. Yet curiously, even if this should turn out to be the case, it will probably be found to illustrate, albeit by a more roundabout route than the one intended, the all-pervading presence of – or at least requirement for – agnosis in our approach to God.

Initially, then, let us interrogate the findings of 'the Preacher' on their own terms: what has he attempted to do, and what, in the process has he discovered? His project is vast. He has devoted himself to study and to the attempt to 'explore by wisdom all that is done under heaven' (1:13). His effort has been thorough. Whatever he has approached he has 'tried to understand' and yet the result is the oft repeated cry that 'All is vanity' – or even more graphically, if more prosaically, in the New International Version of the Bible, 'Everything is meaningless', and the finding of his search is that, 'No-one can comprehend what goes on under the sun. Despite all his efforts to search it out, man cannot discover its meaning. Even if a wise man claims he knows, he cannot really comprehend it' (8:17).

This is true as it stands, and if 8:17 represented the end of Ecclesiastes or was in some way its summation, the book would be an eloquent, if relatively uncomplicated tribute to the necessity for agnosis at the heart of faith.

However, the book's greatness, and its complexity lie precisely in the fact that this is not the case. For the quest goes on, and from agnosis 'the Preacher' moves on again to a sense of renewed meaninglessness in the face of all the apparent (indeed often real) contradictions, injustices and untidinesses of human experience. It is here, in 'vanity', that the book rests, and this 'discovery' of the meaninglessness of all that is (the only possible response to which is awe of God) appears to be the end of the story and the final 'knowledge' attainable by human wisdom.

Herein lies the irony, and the profundity, of Ecclesiastes' exploration of agnosis. For agnosis has been acknowledged and then apparently superseded by a certainty of meaninglessness. Yet the presentation of agnosis at the heart of the book returns to haunt us precisely in the apparent bleakness of its ending – an ending which drives us back into the book in search of something beyond the ending itself, and that something turns out to be the notion of agnosis. For it is as if, in moving beyond acceptance of agnosis, human understanding has at last over-reached itself and can no longer find any meaning even in its glimpses of wisdom. The fact that everything cannot be found out has led to a profound despair (overtly at least) that anything can be found out. And whilst this is where 'the Preacher' ends his discourse, to the reader of the book this is patently not so, for there is so much of real wisdom and beauty in the book which we find ourselves unable simply to dismiss, as 'the Preacher' apparently does, as mere 'vanity'. Our response to 'the Preacher's' searchings is, ironically, almost certain to be different from his own. We cannot close off his search in 'vanity' as he does: instead we find ourselves at the end of the book acknowledging afresh his wisdom along the way, and feeling that beyond this lies not vanity or meaninglessness, but rather the riches of things not yet, or as yet only imperfectly, understood. We find ourselves feeling that Ecclesiastes has just missed glimpsing the possibility of what one might call a 'wisdom beyond wisdom' – a wisdom which does not decline into meaninglessness, but which expands into mystery and silence and wonder in the face of all that is. Perhaps that might even have been the voice of a 'Preacher' less certain than Ecclesiastes of the completeness of his human knowledge; and might it therefore be that Ecclesiastes ironically stands as a tribute not to the 'vanity' of all things, but more simply and yet more profoundly, to the 'vanity' of human certainty – a testament to the value of agnosis as the only way out of the false dilemma of complete knowledge or complete meaninglessness?

Between them, Job, Jonah and Ecclesiastes offer three diverse and mutually enriching perspectives on the place of agnosis in the life of faith, but although they are three of the most distinctive voices they are by no means alone in the pages of the Old Testament. The prophets and psalmists frequently express their bewilderment in the face of God's presence or activity, and there is, as I have remarked elsewhere,[1] particularly in the prophets, an abiding openness to the possibility of new understandings of God and his purposes which indicates that they always felt any present position to be partial and provisional.

Further than this, it would of course be possible to trawl right through the Old Testament in search of every last illustration, but this would add little to the substance of the argument. There is, however, one further episode which deserves consideration here, as it indicates the constancy and integrity with which an attitude of agnosis can be held even *in extremis*. The episode occurs in the book of Daniel, when the three mythical heroes, Shadrach, Meshach and Abednego are about to be thrown into the fiery furnace for failing to worship the golden statue which Nebuchadnezzar has set up. After the three men have been sum-

moned before the king and given their last chance to worship
the statue they reply: 'O Nebuchadnezzar, we do not need to de-
fend ourselves before you in this matter. If we are thrown into
the blazing furnace, the God we serve is able to save us from it,
and he will rescue us from your hand, O king. But even if he
does not, we want you to know, O king, that we will not serve
your gods or worship the image of gold you have set up' (3:16-
18). The key phrase is, of course, 'even if he does not', and its inclusion is a fascinating pointer to the presence of agnosis at the
heart of the Jewish faith. Its inclusion is, in terms of the story,
superfluous. The story is a mythical one anyway, and the author
(and with him the reader) knows full well that the three men are,
as good mythical heroes should be, about to be saved. Why then
gratuitously place this *caveat* in the mouths of Shadrach,
Meshach and Abednego? It is, presumably, to relate a mythical
story to the events of real life in which there is not an omniscient
storyteller there to assure us of a happy ending. However strong
faith may be, there is always the possibility that we may be mistaken, either about God's activity or even about his existence –
and it is in this fundamental awareness of agnosis that we must
live our life, even though alongside it we may decide to stake
our life on God's reality. Agnosis is not a comfortable academic
'armchair option' for when life is going well, but one that is just
as real and just as necessary even – and perhaps especially –
when our faith and our life are most at risk.

Aside from these various characters who either experience or
otherwise illustrate the presence of a radical uncertainty at the
heart of faith, there is running alongside it what might be called
a divine perspective on agnosis whereby God himself is quick to
remind his people that they can never presume to encompass his
fullness. Admittedly there are exceptions to this, such as when
Moses and Aaron, Nadab and Abihu and the seventy elders be-
hold God and eat and drink (Exodus 24:9-11), or when Isaiah receives his call (Isaiah 6:1-8). But these glimpses of God are always presented as 'visual' only, and imply no fullness of understanding. Indeed, in Isaiah's case, the immediate reaction to his

vision is one of unworthiness to have seen it, and there is no pretence of understanding: the prophet is commissioned to bear God's message, but his status remains simply that of a messenger rather than that of a fully understanding partner in the divine communication.

These exceptions aside, then, there are numerous occasions on which God reminds his people that although he is their God and will vouchsafe them as much knowledge of his will as they may need for their direction, yet they must never think to approach the ultimate mystery of his being or his identity: 'I am who I am' is enough to be going on with.

Thus even Moses, to whom this divine name – which thereafter was not even permitted to be spoken or written in full – was revealed, was not allowed to gain full and final access to the reality of God. Moses himself realises the impossibility of this vision and knowledge as he confronts the burning bush, for as soon as God has revealed himself as, 'the God of your Father, the God of Abraham, the God of Isaac and the God of Jacob' (3:6), Moses hides his face because he is 'afraid to look at God'. That this fear is well placed is confirmed later in Exodus as Moses prepares to receive the second set of stone tablets bearing the Ten Commandments. Moses, apparently forgetting his earlier experience, says to God: 'Now show me your glory,' and God replies: 'I will cause all my goodness to pass in front of you, and I will proclaim my name, the Lord, in your presence ... But ... you cannot see my face, for no-one may see me and live' (33:18-20). Thus Moses hides in a cleft in the rock, and God declares that once he has passed by: 'I will remove my hand and you will see my back; but my face must not be seen'(33:23).

Clearly all of this is figurative and mythical language, but through it certain features of our relationship with God are brought into focus. God may be discovered through his attributes (such as goodness) and he may even be named – but simply as sovereign (Lord) and not by any other more revealing appellation. Likewise his presence may be discerned but only retrospectively, and indeed as we shall see throughout this study,

Christian experience is typically of 'God's back' as we recognise him 'after the event'. What is not vouchsafed is access to the absolute and ultimate truth of the being of God: this remains, by divine command, as well as human limitation, a mystery.

These episodes concerning Moses are perhaps the clearest examples of God's own limitation of his self-disclosure, but they are by no means the only ones in the Old Testament. There is, indeed, a close parallel in the experience of Elijah on Mount Horeb in 1 Kings 19, and the account vividly captures the immensity and ultimate unapproachability of the being of God. Elijah shows no reaction to the awesome power of nature in earthquake, wind and fire in which God is not present – these things, however powerful, are within the realm of human knowledge and experience and may be witnessed by ordinary mortals. When he hears the 'gentle whisper' or 'still small voice', however, his reaction is instantaneous: remembering, presumably, the experience of Moses and the divine pronouncement that no-one may see God's face and live, Elijah pulls his cloak over his face before venturing forth to meet the Lord.

Moses and Elijah and with them a few others are, however, privileged individuals, and if even they – who come into the presence of the Lord – may not see him fully revealed, then it is hardly surprising that for the great bulk of the people of Israel the mystery of God is to be approached with even greater circumspection. Always, it seems, there might be one favoured individual who might approach so far, but only so far and no further, but others must remain at a distance. This pattern is plainly in evidence when God says to Moses: 'Go down and bring Aaron up with you. But the priests and the people must not force their way through to come up to the Lord, or he will break out against them' (Exodus 19:24). In essence this same pattern was preserved in the rituals of the temple worship, with one priest chosen by lot from among those on duty to approach the Lord in order to burn incense (cf Matthew 1:8-10). In all of God's dealings with Israel the Old Testament reveals a consistent cognitive and conceptual – though not, vitally, as we shall see, a re-

lational – distance between God and his people, a distance
which is nowhere more poignantly and poetically expressed
than in Isaiah 55: 'For my thoughts are not your thoughts, neither are your ways my ways,' declares the Lord. 'As the heavens
are higher than the earth, so are my ways higher than your
ways, and my thoughts than your thoughts.'

In the experience of the people of Israel, both in general and
as it is either encapsulated or illustrated in certain characters
and stories, and in the persona of God as interpreted and presented in the Old Testament, there is a consistent turning towards agnosis. We have argued already that this is an essential
counter to the often rather anthropomorphic – though brilliantly
colourful – presence of God in Jewish life: that is, story (and the
more dramatic the better) is undoubtedly one of the most effective ways of conveying a message, religious or otherwise, in an
immediately compelling and memorable form, and yet it is impossible to do justice to God simply by presenting him as 'one of
the cast', however central. There needs to be a more reflective
strain running alongside the unfolding drama which allows
God to be – as he must be – larger than the story within which he
is apparently confined.

All of this may be so, but it still does not do full justice to the
fact that agnosis would seem to have been not merely a stylistic
literary device to lend depth to an already powerful and engag-
ing story, but rather something integral to and constitutive of
the whole approach of the Old Testament (and therefore the
Jewish faith) to the religious life. Agnosis is not a secondary fea-
ture of that life, but rather a primary one.

It is necessary that this should be so principally for two reasons, both of which are connected with what we have called the
'relational' nature of the Jewish faith. First, then, there seems to
be a link between the Old Testament authors' concern to present
God as veiling his ultimate identity and the Old Testament pro-
hibition of images or idols. Idols are forbidden not simply because they are inadequate to represent God, but because they
lead to the worshipping of something which is less than the full-

ness of divinity: to be worshipped adequately God may not be
pinned down in any convenient shape, and we pray, as Anselm
recognised much later: 'Not to what I think thou art, but to what
thou knowest thyself to be.'

The position is similar with respect to God's 'identity'. Being
finite and human, no individual or people is capable of assimil-
ating the essence of divinity even were the vision of it to be
vouchsafed to them, and this being the case it is better if they
remain in ultimate ignorance. For what would happen if such a
vision were to be given, which revealed God in all his fullness?
Even if one did 'see God's face and live' it would be inevitable
that over time the 'vision' would become reduced and tamed in
our minds – and therefore in our transmission of it to others –
and yet it would still be surrounded by a now spurious claim to
veracity. The human mind would tame God, and as we shall
argue in a later chapter, the effect of this would actually be to re-
strict him, although this becomes more evident when one begins
to take the incarnation into account. If God is to be free to be
God, then, it appears, he must remain in himself 'beyond' and
unknown. Full knowledge of him would only be appropriate if
human beings had the capacity to live with, assimilate and remain in the presence of the fullness of that knowledge thereafter: as it is, we are not capable of this, and rather than having a
disfigured knowledge of God it is better that his face remain hidden and a genuine agnosis (rather than a false knowledge) become the characteristic mode of our relationship with God. Not
to know God absolutely may be sometimes frustrating, but it allows for a truer relationship with him than a distorted knowledge of him would do.

If the first reason for agnosis being a primary characteristic of
the Jewish approach to faith is concerned with promoting a true
relationship between ourselves and God, then the second reason
in a sense flows from this, and this is that knowing agnosis to be
constitutive of faith allows us to get the priorities of our response to God set in the right perspective and prevents us from
becoming so concerned with our mental imaging and speculation about God that we lose sight of other and more important

aspects of our response to, and relationship with him.

Thus the Old Testament is not – and this is not in any sense to be dismissive of it – so much about trying to understand God as recounting the experience of God and what he has done. The Old Testament is profoundly relational rather than cognitive in its response to God. At one level, as we have seen, God cannot be 'known', or at least nowhere near fully known, but at the level of relationship God is known and responded to with utter commitment. Our understanding may fall short of the reality of God, but our glimpses and glimmerings are still enough for us to respond to the one who has shown us something – even if not everything – of himself, and the quality and commitment of this response is itself far more important than any purely cognitive understanding of God.

Similarly, and it is intimately connected with the notion of relationality rather than cognition, the Jewish response to God was – and perhaps still is, in a way from which we as Christians might well learn – orientated primarily not towards understanding but towards worship. This is not to say that Judaism has never attempted to understand God: it has; but it has also at the same time acknowledged the frailty and provisionality of that understanding and recognised that worship is prior to, and more important than, progress in understanding. Leaving the Old Testament to one side for a moment, this point was precisely and very movingly made in more recent times by a group of rabbis who were, if my memory of the story is correct, prisoners in the concentration camp at Auschwitz. The rabbis decided that God should be put on trial. I forget the exact wording of the charge against him, but it was effectively for crimes against humanity in creating a world in which events like the Holocaust could occur. Following the trial the verdict was pronounced: 'Guilty'; upon which one of the rabbis, noting the hour, reminded the others that it was now time for their evening prayers, and so the essential practice of worship here again took precedence over every other aspect of faith including understanding.

Contrary to initial appearances then, agnosis turns out to be quietly though pervasively present in the pages of the Old Testament and to be a primary factor in shaping the contours of the classical Jewish response to God. It is important next to establish to what extent Christianity has inherited and appropriated this approach, and we therefore turn in the succeeding two chapters first to the New Testament and then to the Christian tradition thereafter, in order to assess the significance of agnosis within the Christian faith as it developed out of its constructively agnostic Jewish heritage.

# CHAPTER 2

# New Testament Agnosis

During the course of our examination of the Old Testament it has become evident that the concept of agnosis, whilst it is sometimes overtly present and is, even at other times, always weaving its way through the text and through the framework of thought behind it like a subterranean but life-giving stream, is nonetheless a kind of trio in a minor key (to use a musical analogy) to the vibrant onward momentum of the scherzo represented by the plethora of impassioned storytelling and characterisation which surrounds it. It is, on the whole, less obvious than the 'and then, and then, and then' of God's acts, and yet it is the bedrock on which any genuinely satisfactory interpretation of those acts must be founded: that is, however much we may seem to have been granted by way of intuition or revelation, still we must be always aware that we have been granted just so much of God's reality as we can bear – and that even then there is the very real possibility that we may have misinterpreted it, either in part or, indeed, entirely.

Agnosis therefore turns out, perhaps to one's initial surprise, to be fundamental to any approach which seeks to do full justice to the complexities of Old Testament thinking about the nature and activity of God. When we turn to the New Testament, though, the case for agnosis looks, on a first approach to the text and its world, to be even less substantial than might have initially appeared to be the case with the Old Testament. This is, I suggest though, not so much because of the evidence of the New Testament itself, but because of the pre-suppositions with which we (naturally enough) approach that text and the expectations which we therefore (equally naturally) read into it. Thus, as

Christians we read the New Testament in certain ways, and it might indeed prove both interesting and instructive to present the New Testament to someone who has never read it before (or if possible never even heard of it) and enquire what they might make of it especially in terms of the concept of agnosis: and we might well be surprised by the results.

Inevitably, then – and in itself this is something to rejoice in rather than repine over – we read (and re-read) the New Testament from the perspective of faith: a faith which we rightly proclaim has brought us life-changing and renewing 'knowledge' of God in and through Jesus Christ. We read the New Testament in the consciousness that at one level, certainly, its 'central theme' is the accessibility of God in Jesus Christ; and reading it with this particular pair of hermeneutical spectacles on, this message of God's accessibility and 'knowability' is the one which we in turn receive from the New Testament. Here, after all, is the story of the incarnation, of God becoming a human being, and what better proof could there be of the accessibility of God than this. Even if we still hold that God cannot be known in himself, here he is, it seems, becoming human that we might know him in this more familiar form.

In one sense this is true enough, but it begs the question of what we mean by 'knowledge' of God (even in Jesus Christ) and blinds us to the fact that agnosis is, in fact, quite compatible with a certain degree of knowledge and with there being a variety of different types or categories of knowledge. We shall argue later in this chapter that the knowledge of God which is imparted through Jesus Christ is principally relational knowledge rather than conceptual or cognitive knowledge, and if this is so then agnosis may perfectly well remain alongside it once we have been enabled to distinguish between the different types of knowledge and allowed ourselves to look again at the familiar stories in the light of these distinctions rather than simply in the light of our own pre-suppositions of knowledge and accessibility.

That this crucial distinction between relational and conceptual knowledge is justified as far as Jesus and the New Testament are concerned is amply borne out by a brief excursus into the realm of patristics, which although it involves a temporary departure from the New Testament itself is instructive because it sheds light on what the first few generations of sub-apostolic Christians made of that text and its central figure, Jesus Christ.

One might expect that if the knowledge of God imparted by Jesus had been cognitive then the theologians of the first few centuries would have had a reasonably easy time of it. Even if Jesus' teaching had been somewhat piecemeal, all that would have been necessary would have been a fairly straightforward task of tidying up and systematising the various pieces of information into a coherent whole. And there would, presumably, in this case, have been relatively little room for dispute – if Jesus had said that such-and-such was definitively so about God, then who would they have been to argue?

When we turn to the reality of the patristic centuries, however, the picture is very different. They patently could not 'read off' the 'facts' of God's essence and nature (or even Jesus') from the teaching of Jesus or from anything else, and their task was immeasurably more complex than this and involved many of the best minds of antiquity in several centuries of debate and, often, of heated controversy.

To begin with, Jesus had not even left them with a neat set of appropriate concepts and categories of thought. True, St John the Evangelist had done his best with the notion of the *Logos*, and a wide variety of titles for Jesus had been left scattered throughout the gospels, but none of it added up to a tidy system of thought, or even, indeed, the beginnings of one. Part of the search, then, was not just for what to say about God and about Jesus in the incarnation, but even how and where to find the right sort of language to say it in, and this was to involve an extensive trawl through the language and concepts of both Greek and Latin philosophy and metaphysics – and even then conceptual confusions were likely to remain between the two languages.

Even once a broad set of concepts and terms had been 'discovered' and had begun to be applied and refined for theological use there was no immediate agreement as to exactly how these were to be interpreted and combined: one nature or two natures; an hypostatic or enhypostatic or anhypostatic union (although the words anhypostatic and enhypostatic were not used as such at the time, the concepts behind them most certainly were); what exactly did *persona* and *prosopon* mean, and so on.

Even in the middle of their most heated disputes as to what it all meant, none of the patristic theologians would have doubted that we are given knowledge of God in Jesus Christ, but in the light of their task they would have been hard pressed to claim that it was in any substantial measure a cognitive knowledge. Patristic theology is, in essence, a conceptual reflection on the experience of relational knowledge, and as such allows an undiminished place for agnosis, both within its own thinking and in the New Testament to which that thinking so consistently refers. If the early fathers could not 'read off' a conceptual knowledge of God from Jesus and the New Testament then no more can we, and we must allow even our deepest probings into divinity (even as revealed and 'known' in Jesus Christ) to remain, as they always will be, provisional and partial.

If we now return to the New Testament itself it may now, in the light of all this, seem less improbable to claim that there are, in fact, plenty of indications in the New Testament that human knowledge and understanding of God – including as he is revealed in Jesus – are fragmentary and limited. Sometimes indeed the gospel writers seem to go out of their way to convey this, albeit usually in an oblique fashion.

One might expect, for example, that since the gospels were all written for the express purpose of bearing witness to faith in Jesus Christ and thereby of strengthening existing faith communities and propagating the spread of the gospel, the various writers would therefore be concerned to tailor (or even, where necessary, re-write) their story in order to maximise its impact and to minimise those elements which reflect less than impressively upon the disciples or which appear to suggest that Jesus' revelation of God is less than immediately transparent.

If anything, however, the opposite appears to be the case. The gospel writers dwell with surprising and apparently unnecessary consistence on the failure of the disciples (and others) to understand substantial amounts of Jesus' teaching and to recognise who he is. Scattered examples of this could be picked more or less at random from any of the gospels: Peter's inability to recognise the significance of Jesus' actions as he washes the disciples' feet (John 13:1-17); the repeated requests of the disciples to Jesus to explain his parables, especially in St Matthew's and St Luke's gospels; their confusion over the 'leaven of the Pharisees and Sadducees' (Matthew 16:5-12); or their obtuseness in discussing who will be the greatest of them even in the context of the Last Supper (Luke 22:24-27). Similar examples could be multiplied almost *ad infinitum* and even by themselves they begin cumulatively to suggest that there might be a reason for so much being made of the disciples' ignorance and blindness.

However, this treatment of the disciples is not merely confined to scattered – and therefore still possibly casual and relatively insignificant – remarks, but is also, and evidently quite deliberately, built into the structure and patterning of the gospels, most clearly so in the case of St Mark's gospel. St Mark may have been – if the general consensus of gospel scholarship is accurate – the earliest of the gospel writers, but he is not any the less a consummate artist for that. Contrary to the teaching of all too many Sunday Schools – and unfortunately clergy and RE teachers also – St Mark's gospel is not a straightforward 'and then, and then, and then' kind of a narrative. It may sometimes appear that way because of its deceptively simple linguistic style, but vocabulary and grammar aside it is a work of rich and complex patterning in which nothing happens by accident. It is – and this is a compliment rather than a disparagement – as much a work of art as it is a proclamation, and its proclamation is all the more powerful because of that.

It is perhaps as well to establish this firmly before building too much upon it, and to look briefly at an example of this artistry which is unrelated to the present argument and in which we therefore have here 'no stake' as it were. Once the principle of Mark's careful organisation of his material is allowed we can then move on to consider an aspect of it which is of more significance in the present discussion.

An apposite instance which springs readily to mind is Mark's treatment of the calling of the first disciples, Peter and Andrew, and James and John, and then later on Levi the tax collector (1:14-20 and 2:13-14). One might well ask why Mark has chosen – for he undoubtedly has chosen and is not constrained by any precise order of events – to arrange these apparently parallel callings so far apart, with the best part of an entire chapter separating them. Would it not have been more logical to have placed the stories together and ended up with a nice neat block of 'calling' pericopes? More logical, perhaps, but far less effective, for Mark achieves something by separating the stories which would not have been possible had they been kept more tidily together. The calling of Peter and Andrew, James and John marks the beginning of Jesus' ministry and sets the tone for it of a calling to personal discipleship and the following of Jesus. Between this and the calling of Levi in the following chapter, however, there occurs a long series of miraculous healings, which by the end of the series threatens to divert attention away from where Jesus ministry began and to present him as a typical *theios aner* or 'divine man' of the type so beloved of Greek antiquity. It is precisely at this point then, that Mark inserts the quintessentially simple and typical calling of Jesus to Levi: 'Follow me,' and in Levi's following we are graphically reminded that whatever else Jesus' ministry may bring, here and nowhere else is the heart of it: in a personal response to a personal call and in the greatest miracle of all – the call and response of love to love.

Furthermore, the fact that this patterning is part of Mark's distinctive religious and artistic genius is further borne out if we notice that neither Matthew nor Luke retains the same structure and that their accounts lose this particular impact in the process. They may possibly be attempting to do different things with their material, but Matthew separates the first two callings from the third (and here it is of Matthew, not Levi) by, amongst other things, the entirety of the Sermon on the Mount, and Luke both places the initial callings later than Mark and complicates it by introducing into it the element of the miraculous. In neither case is the immediacy and power of Mark's account – which owes everything to his religious and aesthetic sense – retained.

We may argue with some justice, therefore, that Mark's gospel is anything but naïve in structure, and that what Mark does by way of patterning he does for a purpose. Nowhere is this more evident than in his amazing treatment of the disciples in an extended passage which runs from 8:22 to 10:52, in which the 'blindness' of the disciples is framed between the healings of two blind men.

The passage opens with the healing of the blind man at Bethsaida, and this is, significantly, a 'two-stage' healing. Initially when the man sees he says, 'I see people; they look like trees walking,' and it is only after Jesus has laid his hands on him for a second time that his sight is completely restored. In a piece of dramatic juxtaposition this is followed immediately by Peter's confession of Jesus as the Christ, which looks like 'sight', but in the light of all that follows we come to conclude that it is, at best, sight like that of the man seeing trees walking!

For between this episode and the healing of blind Bartimaeus the catalogue of the disciples' failings is unmatched anywhere (I think) in any of the gospels. Peter is rebuked by Jesus for not understanding Jesus' prediction of his death; the disciples fail to heal the boy with the evil spirit and then fail to understand Jesus' second prediction of his death; they argue about which of them is the greatest and are rebuked; John tries to stop someone driving out demons in the name of Jesus because he is 'not one of us'; the disciples incur Jesus' indignant anger when they try to prevent little children from coming to him; they are 'amazed' and uncomprehending during Jesus' encounter with the rich young man; and finally James and John ignorantly and arrogantly ask to share the favoured seats with Jesus in his glory. It is at the end of this litany of failure and blindness that Bartimaeus is healed, and significantly we hear that he 'followed Jesus along the road', and we are led to feel that the disciples could learn something about faith and following not merely from Jesus but from this erstwhile blind beggar. It is often, it seems from this account, precisely when we think that we see most clearly that we are in fact most blind! Eyes might be opened more quickly if we would always be a little less certain of the certainty of our own rightness.

This episode, and the general failure of the disciples to 'see' at many points in the gospels provide a pointer – albeit a somewhat oblique one – to a sense within the gospels themselves that human understanding has certain limits when it comes to the 'things of God', and this pointer is made a good deal more explicit when we come to consider the resurrection narratives, which one might think would be – and are often portrayed by the popular mind as being – the most joyfully 'certain' of the gospel stories. In truth, however, this is far from being the case, initially at least. In each of the gospels the simple acceptance of resurrection – let alone any joy in it – is halting, to put it mildly, and taken together across the four gospels the evidence of a stuttering start to resurrection faith is overwhelming.

Mark's gospel, in its original ending, concludes with fear and bewilderment, and indeed with no joy or proclamation whatever: 'They said nothing to anyone because they were afraid' (16:8). Even in its later ending, Mary Magdalene is not believed, nor is the report of the two walking in the country. In Luke's gospel the eleven do not believe the women, 'because their words seemed to them like nonsense' – or in some other versions 'an idle tale' – (24:11), and the two disciples on the road to Emmaeus only finally recognise Jesus after a substantial delay, and then in the highly symbolic breaking of bread. Nor are things much better in St John's gospel, which with its powerful presentation of realised eschatology might be supposed to be the most immediately triumphant in the presence of the resurrection. When the disciples first arrive at the tomb we are told that 'they saw and believed', but in fact what they believed at this point was Mary's news that someone had stolen the body. Their belief, initially, was not in the resurrection at all, a fact which John makes plain when he comments that 'they did not understand from scripture that he must rise from the dead'. Later on in the same gospel, Mary at first supposes Jesus to be the gardener, and Thomas will not believe unless he sees for himself; and finally in St Matthew's gospel, even in the so-called 'great commission' on which so much has since been built, we are almost gratuitously informed that, 'When they saw him they worshipped him; but some doubted' (28:17). Far from there having been instant and joyful certainty, it is a wonder, on the basis of these earliest accounts, that the Christian faith ever took off at all.

The significance of all this is perhaps most clearly demonstrated if we invoke once again the distinction which we have previously drawn between relational and conceptual cognitive knowledge. The disciples had enjoyed a unique and life-enhancing relationship with Jesus during his earthly life and ministry, and therefore one may surmise that when confronted with the resurrection they would passionately have wanted the resurrection to be true and to be more than an illusion or even delusion. So why the hesitation to believe what they must so much have wanted to be true? The reason, I suggest, is actually remarkably simple – the accepted boundaries of cognition. In order to believe in resurrection – even when we want it to be true – we have to break through an enormous barrier of human understanding and, in a sense, allow a negative certainty to become a more positive agnosis. 'Such things,' we may say, 'do not ordinarily happen. But here there appears to be sufficient evidence for me to begin to believe that it may happen, indeed has happened.' The ordinary bounds of human understanding have to be breached in a massive way before we can even begin to 'understand' a happening as shattering as resurrection; and even then, even when we are as we would say 'convinced', agnosis and further limits to our understanding must still remain, because in the face of a phenomenon so foreign to all normal experience, we could yet be wrong, or at least astray in our understanding and interpretation of it. Human cognition is patently, even in the gospels, whose business it is to proclaim it, stretched to its utmost to come to terms with resurrection: to claim absolute cognitive certainty when stretched thus far would be arrogance indeed.

Up to this point we have concentrated largely on the disciples and on their response to Jesus, but it is important to consider in some detail the person of Jesus himself, since much of the evidence for the New Testament vision of a faithful agnosis as an appropriate response to God stems directly from his person and teaching. Admittedly one is at a slight disadvantage here in that what we are presented with in the gospels is a collection of portraits – or perhaps less concretely, portrayals – of Jesus, each of which has already passed through the medium of the passage of time (at least forty years, even in the case of the earliest accounts) and the human mind and spirit in order to reach us in its final form. We do not have access to a direct and, as it were, 'uninterpreted' picture of Jesus in any of the gospels, and there is a considerable amount of disagreement among New Testament scholars as to the degree of historical accuracy with which any or all of the gospel accounts may rightly be credited.

However, this matters less in the present instance than it might do were the issue at stake a different one. It is, I imagine, a reasonably safe assumption that each of the gospel writers wished to render their account of Jesus as lucid and as readily approachable and understandable as possible: there is, after all, little point in proclaiming something obscurely if you can do it more simply. Thus we may assume that the authors of the four gospels did not deliberately set out to muddy the waters of Jesus' teaching. If, therefore, the normal limits of human understanding or knowledge are breached in that teaching we may reasonably conclude that that this accurately enough reflects the nature – even if not necessarily the precise wording – of Jesus' teaching. Furthermore, the issue at stake does not depend upon the exact verbal accuracy of individual pieces of teaching, but upon the whole style and tenor of Jesus' teaching ministry – about which there seems to be adequate agreement that the gospels provide a substantially reliable picture.

Thus aside from particular statements in the mouth of Jesus to which one would not necessarily attribute too much historical accuracy, especially when they emanate from St John's gospel (such as, 'No one has seen the Father except the one who is from God', [6:46]), there are, much more significantly, three aspects of Jesus' teaching style which indicate that a response to God is not simply – indeed not at all – a matter of cognitive certainty but must contain a genuine measure of agnosis.

The first of these concerns simply the characteristic form of Jesus' teaching – the parable. Certainly it is true that this is not the only form in which Jesus' teaching is couched: there are, for example, substantial passages of the Sermon on the Mount or John's discourses which are much more directly didactic or ex-hortatory, but the parable is unmistakably the most distinctive form of Jesus' teaching, and it is equally the form which most people remember best.

More importantly, though, the parables often function as a dramatic or pictorial way of overturning all human assump-tions. Again one could choose examples almost at random, but two typical instances might be the parable of the sheep and the goats (Matthew 25:31-46), which radically re-evaluates what faith and discipleship are about and includes the possibility that they may even be wholly unconscious, and the parable of the workers in the vineyard (Matthew 20:1-16) which disturbingly calls into question all of our human notions of fairness and jus-tice when weighed in the scales against divine generosity. Similarly, another function of the parables is frequently to ex-plore an idea in story and image which perhaps could not be so satisfactorily explored in any more direct way. So it is, for exam-ple, with the three linked parables of loss and redemption in Luke fifteen, or the various parables concerning the kingdom of heaven such as those likening it to a mustard seed or yeast in a batch of dough (Luke 13:18-21).

Apart from their value as a readily memorable teaching aid, Jesus' choice of the parable as his most distinctive teaching form would appear to say something about the nature of that teaching itself. There is, it appears, no satisfactory way in which the 'things of God' can be rendered into straightforward conceptual and cognitive terms – as successive generations of comment-ators and preachers have frequently discovered to their cost when they attempt to explain precisely what a particular para-ble 'means'. What a parable 'means' is usually the parable itself which defies any more precise rendering in conceptual lang-uage. It was, I think, Schumann, who when asked what a partic-ular piece 'meant' said, 'It means this,' and sat down at the piano and played the piece through once again.

Everything is by picture or by analogy, and the parables therefore seem to reflect the fact that everything that we 'know' of God is of this analogous and pictorial nature, and is therefore only an approximation to a reality which, whilst we may be able partially and fleetingly to imagine or glimpse it pictorially, we can never capture in any more absolute or precise cognitive in-tellectual terms. The choice of parable rather than propositional statement as a teaching method itself indicates the extent to which unknowing – and knowing anything at all only by imper-fect analogy – is the distinctive idiom of faith.

The second aspect of Jesus' teaching style which is relevant here flows directly from his employment of this parabolic and non-cognitive form, and this is the purpose of his teaching: what it was that he was concerned to impress upon his disciples and the gathering crowds. Thus, neither in form nor in content is Jesus' teaching primarily oriented towards the imparting of pre-cise propositional knowledge. Nowhere does Jesus launch into a metaphysical discussion of God's essence or of the nature of his own Sonship, and indeed quests for 'knowledge' of this sort are usually closed off by Jesus on the grounds that 'No one knows', or 'No one has seen' except the Father himself. Such knowledge is not only inappropriate for us, but unavailable to us.

Instead of this then, Jesus' teaching is directed towards two things: a faithful and relational following of Jesus, and a particu-lar way of life which such a following entails. So we are directed towards a God who loves us, forgives us, knows us, judges us and so on, and is primarily 'known' to us as the Father of the Son and therefore by extension, or more properly by adoption, our Father also, and this 'knowledge' is experiential rather than conceptual.

This relationship is then, in turn, expressed in a way of life, such indeed that the early Christians were known as followers of 'the Way', and never as followers of 'a system'. This way of life is rooted in the twin concerns of worship and ethics, both of which are substantially reflected in Jesus' teaching and which mutually interpenetrate and inform one another, and both of which reflect also the pre-eminently relational nature of our faith: worship is the common experience of Christians which unites them in communion both 'vertically' with God and 'horizontally' with one another; and an ethical approach to life is, from a Christian point of view, one which recognises that, in various ways, we care for one another not primarily because it is 'commanded' or because we may be judged if we do not, but because we are together children of the one Father and therefore, in a sense which is far more than just symbolic, brothers and sisters to one another. And all of this may be experienced as true, and indeed as we would say, be 'known' to be true, without this involving any conceptual certainty as to how (metaphysically or propositionally) it comes to be true. Agnosis remains a reality, and the fact that the content of Jesus' teaching does little or nothing to dispel it suggests that it must, if we are to be faithful to that teaching, continue to remain so.

Thus neither the distinctive form nor the overall tone of the content of Jesus' teaching professes to offer any propositional certainty in the realm of faith, and the same implicit understanding of an agnostic faith is presented by the models which Jesus chooses as being exemplars of that faith. Very often he points to the unlikely and the unlearned as being those in whom faith (and with it 'knowledge' of and relationship with God) is most real and most effective: the poor widow; the publican as opposed to the Pharisee; the 'sinful' woman' in preference to Simon the Pharisee and so on. In doing this Jesus is clearly not (and no more so are we here) against learning as such. All of his teaching reveals him to have been well-versed in the Jewish scriptures, and to be, in many respects, a 'typical' rabbi. Yet at the same time Jesus is plainly opposed to learning when it becomes the touchstone of faith and becomes more important than a prior relationship with God: knowing God is, and must be, always prior to knowing about God.

This is further reflected in Jesus' consistent calling of the disciples to humility, and his pointing to examples of humility, and perhaps pre-eminently in his frequent use of children as examples of the kingdom of heaven, both in terms of needing to become as little children in order to receive or 'inherit' the kingdom of heaven, and in the context of the dire warnings against causing 'one of these my little ones' to sin. Admittedly there has been much sentimental nonsense written – and yet more spoken, no doubt, in countless emotive sermons – about the gorgeousness and innocence of little children (which tends to put one off them!), but sentimentality is not Jesus' concern in his teaching about them. Little children can be as nasty and spiteful as any adult – indeed more so than most adults! – so it is not for their supposed 'angelic' qualities that Jesus commends them. It is, I believe, instead for their patent and arresting quality – whether they are 'nice' or 'nasty', and so the danger of sentimentality is avoided – of 'unknowing' and bewilderment. Very often they simply do not know: they are amazed, stunned and therefore also delighted or downcast by life. There is a rawness of response to life which a more cognitive and analytical approach misses. What Jesus is pointing to and holding up as a model is this rawness – or perhaps freshness is a better word – of response to God, which relies on knowing that we do not know and therefore cannot explain everything. Children grow up and can become cynical as they 'know' things: if this is the end of faith (in which we only think we 'know' things) then woe betide us, especially if we impart this deadness to any other of God's children.

St Paul may have adversely contrasted the knowledge of

children and adults (and admittedly he was trying to make a very different point), but Jesus might well have pointed out that children at least react with delight to what they see in a mirror (which image, as St Paul uses it, is itself a profound admission of agnosis), and that the longer we can go on avoiding putting such fundamentally religious childlike ways behind us, the better. Agnosis is not only a reality of the adult world, but a positive religious benefit which allows us access to what Michael Mayne so poignantly describes as 'a kind of reverent and infectious wonder'.[1] This infection of wonder is the legacy of Jesus' teaching, and yet it is only agnosis that will enable us to catch it. Agnosis may be presented on the whole obliquely in the New Testament, but it is firmly embedded at its heart nonetheless.

# CHAPTER 3

# *Agnosis in Christian Experience*

During the course of our exploration of the New Testament we have already considered, even if only briefly, the theological experience of the patristic centuries and established that even their powerfully conceptual approach to faith, which resulted in such enduring and memorable formulations of the doctrines of the faith, was not immune from agnosis. Indeed a measure of agnosis was seen to be implicit in the execution of a project so vast, and one might well argue that at certain of the points at which the Fathers were in danger of running aground, it was an excess of over-certainty and the consequent egress of agnosis and humility which engendered the impasse.

A similar conclusion might well be drawn as we come to consider the broad outlines of theological and church history across the centuries; namely that agnosis, whilst surfacing vividly – and refreshingly – from time to time, especially in certain periods and in particular individuals, has generally been paid insufficient attention. Furthermore, the deeper one goes in one's delving through the centuries, the clearer it becomes that this marginalising of agnosis has been, sometimes directly and sometimes indirectly, the cause of (or at least a significant factor in) many of the church's severest problems. Indeed, I would argue strenuously that this is still the case today, and that as Maurice Wiles has cogently remarked in a particularly perceptive article:

> … insistence on a strong dose of agnosticism as an essential component in Christian belief and commitment is admittedly not common currency in the life of the churches. But that is a sign of their weakness, not of their strength.[1]

For all that, though, whilst it may often have been pushed to the sidelines, agnosis has never entirely disappeared from the consciousness either of church life in general or of theology in particular. It has been kept alive in the thinking of a variety of influential individuals and movements down the ages. It would be quite possible to write an entire book tracing this line of descent, and it would undoubtedly prove fascinating to turn over many of the 'living stones' of the church's past to see what lies concealed underneath them. Here, however, it is sufficient simply to select a few individuals and schools of thought to indicate that agnosis, however neglected it may at times have been, has a long and honourable history at the heart of Christian life and thought.

Although we have touched on the patristic era in the previous chapter it seems appropriate to revisit the period here at least in passing, since there is one figure in particular who seems to encapsulate within himself both the power and depth of patristic conceptual thought and also a profound acknowledgement of ultimate agnosis which runs alongside this in a way which is complementary to it rather than in conflict with it. That figure is St Augustine of Hippo. At a first glance he might seem rather an unlikely candidate for the role of champion of the cause of agnosis, for in an age of controversy Augustine was more outspoken than most, especially in his long-running disputes with Pelagius over grace and free will, and with the Donatists. Not surprisingly his controversial and polemical works show few traces of an agnostic outlook, for in these works he was concerned to refute certain specific positions which the Catholic Church (rather than just Augustine himself) defined as erroneous or heretical. His celebrated *Confessions* are, however, a different matter. Here Augustine is intimate and reflective rather than outward-looking and combative, and the work betrays a spirit which, however rarely it might appear in the heat of controversy, was nonetheless clearly foundational for the way in which Augustine perceived his faith. There are moments in the *Confessions* when Augustine emerges as a poet as well as a theologian of genius, and there is one such episode which captures the perception of agnosis almost perfectly, as it swings back and forth between the attempt to say something of God and the acknowledgement that whatever we say our words are inadequate, and that in the end we remain in the dynamic tension of being able to say nothing and yet having to try to say something. The passage occurs early in Book One and therefore sets the tone for the rest of Augustine's spiritual autobiography. The passage is lengthy but deserves full quotation, especially in the resonant translation of the Tractarian scholar, Edward Pusey:

> What art Thou then, my God? What, but the Lord God? *For who is Lord but the Lord? or who is God save our God?* Most highest, most good, most potent, most omnipotent; most merciful, yet most just; most hidden, yet most present; most beautiful, yet most strong; stable, yet incomprehensible; unchangeable, yet all-changing; never new, never old ... ever working, ever at rest; still gathering, yet nothing lacking; supporting, filling, and overspreading; creating, nourishing, and maturing; seeking, yet having all things. Thou lovest, without passion; art jealous, without anxiety; repentest, yet grievest not; art angry, yet serene; changest Thy works, Thy purpose unchanged; receivest again what Thou findest, yet didst never lose; never in need, yet rejoicing in gains; never covetous, yet exacting usury. Thou receivest over and above, that Thou mayest owe; and who hath aught that is not Thine? Thou payest debts, owing nothing; remittest debts, losing nothing. And what have I now said, my God, my life, my holy joy? or what saith any man when he speaks of Thee? Yet woe to him that speaketh not, since mute are even the most eloquent.[2]

In his more polemical works, Augustine sometimes appears to see things rather too much in black and white, but he is revealed here as a thinker who was well acquainted – in his personal faith even if not always in his public pronouncements – with the more finely shaded tones which our condition of unknowing entails.

During the course of this survey we shall maintain a proper chronological sequence, but examples will be drawn from a wide range of cultural and denominational backgrounds, reflecting the fact that this is a personal selection of figures and movements which seem to me to be significant, and is not intended to be in any way definitive or exhaustive.

With this proviso, we may now move across cultures, from the dominant Graeco-Roman world of the patristic era to the almost equally influential world of what is broadly called Celtic Christianity of the sixth to ninth centuries, these centuries being, although it extended in its distinctive form both before and after these dates, the period of its most distinguished flowering.

Admittedly one approaches the world of Celtic Christianity with a good deal of caution today, for it has been romanticised, idealised and held to be representative of such a wide range of spiritual and theological values that, as Oliver Davies and Fiona Bowie tartly declare, it has become a 'field which abounds with popular representations and misrepresentations,' such that, 'it can become increasingly difficult to tell fact from fiction.'[3]

In the midst of all the distortions and misconceptions, there are though two characteristic traits in the literature of the Celtic Church which betoken the presence of a genuine agnosis as a living part of that church's faith.

The first of these is the perception, central to any understanding of the Celtic Church, of the church as a 'pilgrim people' and of faith itself as a pilgrimage. This perception is reflected not only in the literature but also extensively in the practice of the Celtic Church which found expression both in pilgrimages *per se*, and also in an extraordinary degree of missionary enterprise in which the missionary was always perceived as a type of *peregrinatio*. This use of pilgrimage as a governing metaphor for the Christian life conveys the idea of an intense and continuous searching as being a primary constituent of faith, and the characters held up as exemplars, such as St Patrick, St Columba and Brendan the Navigator, serve powerfully to reinforce this notion. Faith is not a ready-made package simply to be received whole, but something to be sought for more and more fully over a lifetime, and of which there is, therefore, by definition, always something more to be discovered, thus making our present situation and knowledge (whatever that may happen to be) always incomplete and provisional. Nor is there any need to burrow through some of the more arcane recesses of Celtic literature to discover works which exhibit precisely this sense of onward searching and accompanying longing for God. A very simple old Irish poem rendered into a hymn speaks movingly of the soul's desire to see God both here and hereafter, and concludes with a verse which expresses this intention throughout the whole of life – faith being a 'project' which will take this long to reach completion:

> This still my soul's desire
> Whatever life afford,
> To gain my soul's desire
> And see thy face, O Lord.[4]

Secondly, and running alongside this vision of longing pilgrimage, Celtic spirituality is distinctive – though not unique – in holding together in a creative tension and balance a very strong sense of the presence of a firmly Trinitarian God in all things, together with an accompanying – and equally powerful – sense of awe and mystery in the face of the majesty and unknowability of that same God. Again, a simple hymn, this time attributed to St Columba, provides ample evidence. Each of the two parts of the hymn ends with an ascription of praise to the Trinity, and in the course of the first part of the hymn, which extols the majesty and great deeds of God, verse seven reads:

> Beyond our ken thou shinest,
> The everlasting light;
> Ineffable in loving,
> Unthinkable in might.[5]

One feels that across cultures and languages and centuries, Augustine might well have joined in the final 'Amen'!

So too, from a later century, would St Thomas Aquinas, although, like Augustine he may appear a surprising choice: there
is, after all, something potentially paradoxical in suggesting that
one of theology's greatest 'systematisers' should appear as a
major contributor to the place of unknowing in theology.
However, not only did Aquinas speak of his magnificent theological productions as being merely 'straw', but far more importantly the entirety of his theological thinking has, as one of its primary tenets, the unknowability of God, the absoluteness of
which is expressed as forcibly as one could wish by Herbert
McCabe: ' ... God is wholly unintelligible to us. We have no idea
what God is.'[6] It is in the context of this unknowing that
Aquinas' thinking comes to birth and, in the light of his comment about straw, it is also where that thinking comes to rest,
very much as Augustine's thinking about God had done eight
hundred years previously.

Separated from Aquinas by a century or so, but influenced –
as was almost all European religious thought from the early
thirteenth century at least until the Council of Trent – by the
world of Aquinas' thought, even if not necessarily by its detailed
presentation, were the medieval mystics. This period from
around the fourteenth century to the sixteenth century was not,
of course, the only period in history which has witnessed an up-
surge in mysticism, and mystics have always emerged and presumably always will emerge, in every age, as John Macquarrie
has recently and illuminatingly reminded us.[7] The medieval
period is remarkable, however, in the range and quality of the
literature exploring mystical experience which it spawned in
several great centres, perhaps most notably England, Germany
and Spain.

At the beginning of the period then, there came the delicate
flowering of English mysticism, whose spirit is most perfectly
and characteristically captured by the anonymous author of *The
Cloud of Unknowing*. The very title of this book is, of course, itself
significant, and the central premise of the treatise is that one
must enter the cloud of unknowing before one can begin to

experience the intensity of God's love and presence which tran-
scends understanding. All that is known must be left behind in
order to open us to the presence of the one who is 'unknown'
and yet experienced. This process is delightfully depicted in a
passage from chapter six, the ending of which, even if not the
entire passage, will be familiar to many:

> But now you will ask me, 'How am I to think of God himself,
> and what is he?' and I cannot answer you except to say 'I do
> not know!' For with this question you have brought me into
> the same darkness, the same cloud of unknowing where I
> want you to be! For though we through the grace of God can
> know fully about all other matters, and think about them –
> yes, even the very works of God himself – yet of God himself
> can no man think. Therefore I will leave on one side every-
> thing I can think, and choose for my love that thing which I
> cannot think! Why? Because he may well be loved, but not
> thought. By love he can be caught and held, but by thinking
> never.[8]

Drawing on this same sense of absolute unknowing, but exploring it in a more schematic and arguably an altogether deeper
way, St John of the Cross finds radical unknowing to be the beginning of illumination. As Rowan Williams observes in his
masterly study of Christian spirituality: 'Illumination is the run-
ning-out of language and thought, the compulsion exercised by
a reality drastically and totally beyond the reach of our conceptual apparatus.'[9] As one goes deeper into this very distinctive
spirituality one discovers that much has been written by way of
commentary on the 'Dark night of the soul' in particular, and yet
it remains a notoriously difficult concept to grasp – unless, I suppose, one happens to have experienced it for oneself – but it
seems to be the case that at least a part of this experience is the
letting go of illusory 'certainties' which are then replaced with a
faithful unknowing which places itself more humbly, because of
its emptiness, in the hand of God. This experience may be profoundly painful as well as ultimately liberating, because once

supposed 'certainties' have been shed, God may be experienced for a time as absent or even as hostile, but even this absence is to be welcomed as being truer than any more comfortable illusion:

> In suffering they [the mystics] are aware, though not in an emotionally satisfying way, which would neutralise the pain, that they are more in the truth, closer to reality and thus to God. They prefer to feel the utter emptiness of everything, the desolation and the futility of life, rather than be fed with what is not him.[10]

Agnosis is not so much simply a component of the mystical tradition, but the essence of it, and it is only in the darkness of radical unknowing that God can be most profoundly met and experienced.

As well as being central to some of the deepest understandings of spirituality, agnosis has always continued to be essential – as we saw in the cases of Augustine and Aquinas – to any genuinely open and creative theological method. Admittedly these qualities have not always been in evidence, especially in eras of controversy, but there have been at least two distinct periods in the history of the Anglican Church – as there have equally been times in the histories of other churches – when this open-minded agnosis has flourished most profusely. The first is that of the great Anglican divines of the late sixteenth and seventeenth centuries, and the second is what one might call the *Lux Mundi* phenomenon of the late nineteenth century.

The names of the great Anglican divines – Hooker, Jewel, Taylor *et al* – are certainly very familiar, but perhaps the magnitude of their achievement is not always fully appreciated. And at least a part of their distinctive genius lies in their commitment to a balance between positive statement and an underlying agnosis about the deepest matters. That this was achieved so consistently was all the more remarkable given the circumstances and period in which they thought and wrote. The age was one of controversy, especially during the time of the earlier writers such as Hooker, when the Church of England had only recently emerged from the savage religious to-ing and fro-ing of the reigns of Henry VIII and Mary Tudor into the relatively calm waters of Elizabethan England, and of course during the seventeenth century there would then be the rise of Puritanism, the Commonwealth and the Restoration to be faced.

It would therefore have been entirely understandable, if regrettable, if these thinkers had attempted to produce a rigidly defined confessional structure for the Church of England which provided neat boundaries and a satisfyingly clear and confessionally exclusive interpretation of all possible controversial points of doctrine. It is to their eternal credit that these great thinkers of the period attempted to do nothing of the sort. Certainly they aimed to be definite whenever possible – in matters of church practice, government, methods of approach to scripture, theological reasoning and so on. But at the same time they never 'closed off' their theology at all points, or claimed too high a place for human reason in the face of divinity. This is particularly evident in Hooker's work, as we saw in the introduction to this volume, and it is summed up with a feeling of sympathetic delight by Michael Ramsey, who himself in his life and writings shared something of the spirit of these great figures:

> A sense of mystery and of the mysteriousness of divine truth is something Hooker felt very strongly indeed. Again and again we find him pausing and saying, 'Do not ask me to define it, do not define it yourself, it really is truly mysterious.'[11]

For Hooker, and indeed for the later divines also, agnosis was both a necessary response to this sense of mystery and also an essential pre-requisite for the appropriate maintenance of it.

The situation was, to all outward appearances, very different two hundred years after Hooker during the middle and later years of the nineteenth century, but the temptations to defensiveness and an unyielding aggressiveness in theology were in fact not dissimilar, although the spurs to such behaviour had indeed changed. Thus just as the theologians of the late sixteenth and seventeenth centuries might have reacted negatively and defensively to the politics and vicissitudes of church life in the period, so too theology in the mid to late nineteenth century was under pressure, not this time from governments or confessional unrest among the churches, but from the findings of other academic disciplines than theology, most notably the sciences and the growth of a relativising sense of history.

In large measure the church had not initially responded with either courage or flexibility to this challenge, and the mid-Victorian years witnessed a widespread and widely documented crisis of faith which was accentuated by the new growth of historical biblical criticism and by the publication of Darwin's *The Origin of Species* in 1859.

In this climate the achievement of Charles Gore and the *Lux Mundi* group in 1889 appears all the more remarkable. For in this one volume the Church of England began to come to terms with, and even to view positively, many of the developments which had previously appeared to be so threatening, such as, to single out only one example, the theory of evolution which was addressed by Aubrey Moore's essay on 'The Christian Doctrine of God'. Any such rapport with the prevailing scientific and historical culture would have been remarkable enough in itself, but what is most extraordinary about the *Lux Mundi* group – and it is probably also why their work has proved so enduring in terms of method, even once the precise content had begun to become dated – is the means by which this new relationship with the surrounding culture was forged. For the *Lux Mundi* theologians showed a spiritual courage of a rare kind. Instead of restating (or even cleverly re-working) the positions of an earlier age, they found the nerve and wisdom to allow all manner of previously hallowed certainties to fall away, leaving them to face, in a genuinely agnostic faith, the discoveries and theories of their own generation. Learning the way of unknowing, as the *Lux Mundi* contributors proved, is at once as essential, and as potentially painful as it is life-giving, for the theologian as it is for the mystic.

Finally, and curiously, in this dash across the centuries, this discovery – or rediscovery – of the *Lux Mundi* thinkers is as relevant today as it was over one hundred years ago. In a sense unknowing becomes more and more important the greater our knowledge itself becomes, and in the twentieth and twenty-first centuries one can trace two separate strands of thought which in their mixture of convergence and conflict bear this out. Thus for much of the twentieth century the intellectual world was dominated by a scientific – or perhaps pseudo-scientific is a better term – scepticism and rationalism which has questioned, and indeed frequently dismissed, the value of anything which cannot be 'proved' in at least quasi-scientific terms. In philosophy the most glaringly obvious example of this would be the reign (even if it was only a short-lived one) of logical positivism, but the same tendency could be found in other disciplines also. Knowledge, to this way of thinking, is everything, and consists of that which can be verified: all else is either non-existent or simply meaningless nonsense.

More recently, however, science itself has been in the forefront of a revolution against such an attitude. As the sciences have discovered more and more about ourselves and about the universe in which we live, a remarkable thing has happened. Many scientists, including among them eminent ones in very different fields, such as John Polkinghorne, Arthur Peacocke and John Habgood, have acknowledged and rejoiced in a renewed sense of mystery at the heart of their work. Beyond whatever is known stands the entire mystery of all that is, God included, and God has, not coincidentally, found himself firmly back on the philosophical and metaphysical agenda for the first time in fifty years. The sense of mystery is, paradoxically, fostered by expanding knowledge: it is a classic example of the old adage, 'The more you know, the more you know you don't know.' Agnosis in scientific and intellectual thinking in general has once again, after a period out in the wilderness, made room in the bed for the complementary agnosis which is the hallmark of all authentic theology.

This survey has been necessarily brief and will inevitably have been personal and therefore partial, but enough has been said to indicate that as a concept and as a positive theological and spiritual value, agnosis has a long and readily traceable history throughout the centuries of Christianity. At the beginning of this chapter we remarked that whilst always present, the notion of agnosis has frequently been pushed to the margins of Christian life, and that this has contributed to many of the most serious crises in the life of the church. It now remains, therefore, in the latter part of this chapter, to return to this remark and to flesh it out somewhat, and in so doing to begin to highlight the enduring – and hence also contemporary – significance of agnosis both for the Christian faith *per se* and for its reflection and vitality in the institutional church.

It may seem strange – almost paradoxical – on first sight at least, to suggest that too much certainty has been, and continues to be, bad for the church, but that is precisely what we are arguing here, and it would appear to be true both as far as the church's internal affairs are concerned and in its relationship with the world around it.

This history of the church, then, is littered with schisms, whether great or small, right from its earliest days. The overt cause of these schisms has ranged over almost every conceivable point of doctrine (and a few fairly inconceivable ones also!) and church practice, and this has tended to obscure one fundamental similarity between most, if not indeed all of them. This is simply that whilst it may be true that one person or group favours one practice or doctrinal interpretation and another faction prefers an alternative practice or viewpoint, this does not necessarily lead to schism and mutual anathema. The factor which produces schism is a conviction of inflexible and unshakeable 'rightness' on the part of those involved which leads either to one group being 'expelled' from fellowship by the other, or to one group feeling the requirement to break away from the other to form a new ecclesial identity which is perceived as being purer or better than that which has been left behind. It is, in a

very real sense, 'knowledge' – in this case both knowledge of a
particular position and the consequent conviction of its 'rightness' – which produces schism. Hooker's remark (although one
might wish to change its precise terms of reference today) is as
apposite now as it was three hundred or so years ago: 'Two
things there are that trouble these latter times: one is that the
Church of Rome cannot, another is that Geneva will not, err.' A
little knowledge may be a dangerous thing, but the conviction of
a lot of knowledge is infinitely more so. Given that there have
been points where a different and more open course has pre-
vailed, one wonders what the history of Christianity might have
looked like had there been, throughout that history, a more consistent welcoming of agnosis and of a consequent humility especially in periods and areas of concern in which opinions differed
most sharply. The church might still not have remained whole
and entirely undivided, but one might hazard a guess that it
would, at the very least, have been considerably less fragmented
than is, sadly, the case today.

Secondly, if 'rightness' has plagued the church in terms of its
own internal relations, then it has equally bedevilled what
might be called the 'foreign policy' of the church – that is, its relationship with the culture and general intellectual and social
ethos which surrounds it at any given time.

We have seen already that whilst there has always been a
thread of unknowing running through the history of the church,
yet this has not often been at the centre of the church's 'official'
or institutional life. Thus for the most part the church's 'official'
response to cultural and intellectual developments has been to
judge them in the light of its own convictions, and in the accompanying a priori assumption (or perhaps determination) that
those convictions are themselves of a different and superior
'rightness' to the discoveries or insights of any other area of
thought. As 'Queen of the Sciences' theology has often been very
quick to attempt to ensure that those whom she has seen as her
courtiers remain in their proper (and inferior) places. The problem, of course, has been – and it has occurred with increasing

frequency during the past four hundred years or so – that time has all too often proved the church to have been flatly and embarrassingly wrong in its reaction when confronted with scientific discoveries in particular. Contrary to the church's initial – and fairly sustained – opinion, the earth did truly turn out to revolve around the sun; evolution does appear to provide a broadly credible account of the development of life on earth; until and unless a better theory is found, the 'big bang' does seem to offer a coherent framework for the beginning of the universe, and so on. In each case, though, theology and the church have had to work very hard to catch up the ground lost at the very beginning through their first negative response to a set of new ideas which called into question – or at least demanded a reinterpretation of – convictions which were felt to be the church's own sacrosanct ones which might not be tampered with or trespassed on by others. Time and again the church has forfeited its credibility as the price of clinging on to supposed 'knowledge', and just as with the history of its various schisms, one wonders whether less certainty and more flexibility might have proved a strength rather than a weakness in the church: the inflexible brittleness of cast iron might conceivably have been refined into the finer suppleness of steel.

In the course of this chapter, then, we have traced the existence of, and highlighted the enduring need for agnosis through the centuries. Through this and through our exploration of the deeply biblical roots of agnosis a substantial case has been made to suggest that the concept is not a new or threatening one, (the concept of agnosis far pre-dating T. H. Huxley's nineteenth century coining of the term 'agnostic', which is itself so often misapplied as to be today thoroughly misleading) but is theologically and spiritually 'respectable', and we may now therefore turn to the issue of its identity and necessity in the church and in the theology of the present day.

# CHAPTER 4

# The Meaning of Agnosis for Today

Thus far we have traced at least something of the history of the way of unknowing in Christianity, but it is important at this stage to examine in some detail what the concept might mean in a present day context. As we do this it is essential to ensure that the 'content' and implications of agnosis are understood as clearly as possible, for it is, unfortunately, a term which may all too easily be misinterpreted depending upon whatever set of presuppositions (many of which may well be false or misleading) we may bring to it. It may be, as we have earlier acknowledged, that the idea of unknowing may seem to some, for a variety of reasons, to be a disturbing or threatening one. It is therefore the intention in the present chapter to indicate that this is not the case, and to delineate as transparently as possible both what agnosis is and, equally importantly, what it is not.

There is in particular one potentially confusing corpus of ideas which must be dispensed with before agnosis can be viewed without unhelpful preconceptions, and the sooner this is done the better. Mention was made at the end of the previous chapter of T. H. Huxley's nineteenth century coining of the term 'agnostic', and it is unfortunately the case that what is now 'received opinion' about the meaning of agnostic is likely to colour our perception of agnosis. To be fair to Huxley, the word 'agnostic' was, in its first appearance and use morally and spiritually neutral – to be agnostic was simply to acknowledge that one did not know. Since then, however, the term has gathered to itself a wide variety of negative overtones such that the meaning of the word in its original sense has been all but lost: it is rather like the hull of a boat which we know to be there somewhere but whose appearance and even shape has been disfigured by an unchecked growth of barnacles.

Thus a dictionary may still provide an accurate definition, but if asked to define 'agnostic' the majority of people would probably come up with something a good deal more 'value-laden' than simply one who does not know. For in popular usage the term now has powerful overtones of scepticism, and a feeling that not only can we not know but there is no point in trying to know – and very often indeed, in religious usage, people who describe themselves as being agnostic may well mean that they cannot be bothered to think because they cannot see any point in doing so. Genuine agnosticism is very rare indeed, and more often than not the word is actually wrongly (and deeply misleadingly) employed to mean nothing more than a negatively-charged spiritual laziness. Agnosis, it must be forcefully said, has nothing whatever to do with this prevalent but corrupt and degraded use of 'agnostic' -- although clearly it does have a good deal more in common with Huxley's original meaning of the word.

Furthermore, agnosis is not intended to convey any sort of declaration that we can do nothing in the way of knowledge, or to suggest that attempting to know does not matter. Quite simply, it does matter very much indeed. Out of our attempts to know more clearly about God have come all of the rich insights of doctrine and the depth of spirituality of the Christian church across the ages which have brought life and hope (and entirely changed and renewed lives) to millions. Clearly this cannot and should not be dismissed or in any way disparaged. Agnosis is not a back door for any more corrosive influence. It simply guards us against falling into the trap of certainty which is liable to distort our vision of God and his will and may even, as we shall argue later, threaten to thwart his purposes. In contrast to any such sense of certainty – and it will, by definition, be a false certainty anyway – agnosis simply acknowledges and reminds us at every turn of the radical provisionality and inadequacy of every human attempt to know God, at least conceptually.

If agnosis needs to be distinguished from the negative overtones of 'agnostic' and brought into a right relationship with the
original meaning of the term, then it equally needs to be clearly
related to the two classical methods of theology, the cataphatic
and apophatic, or positive and negative ways. Again there are
some fine distinctions to be drawn if the nature of agnosis is to
be most accurately and helpfully understood.

Thus it might be presumed that agnosis is to be identified
with the negative way, but as we understand agnosis here, this
is not, in fact, the case, although it is obviously closely allied to it.
The apophatic or negative way in theology proclaims that nothing can rightly be said of God because he is beyond any of our
concepts and words. This, of course, is no more than might be
said from a position of thoroughgoing agnosis. However, it is
generally held – and almost unfailingly so in the Eastern theological tradition – that the apophatic way lies 'beyond' and is in
some absolute way 'higher' than the cataphatic way. That is,
once we have tried to understand God in language and concept
and in relationship to the things of this world which we do more
clearly know, we pass beyond this stage as we discover its inadequacy and enter, like Moses, a kind of divine darkness in which
we are exposed to the absolute 'otherness' of God. Furthermore,
once we have reached this point and discovered the apophatic
way there is no turning back, for the unsophisticated positive
assertions of the cataphatic way are no longer adequate or spiritually satisfying.

It is at this point that agnosis parts company, to a degree at
least, with the apophatic tradition. Certainly the inadequacy of
positive statement about God is recognised, but there is no accompanying sense that saying nothing or trying to speak of God
in a negative way is any more appropriate, and certainly not that
it is 'better' than a more positive approach. Agnosis, although it
may share much with the apophatic tradition, cannot be wholly
identified with it, and it stands rather as a kind of meeting place
between the two great theological methods. There is a point of
return from the 'divine darkness', and as Augustine discovered,

although we can strictly speaking say nothing of God, yet we are compelled again and again to try, for only so can we gain any glimpses of who he might be or give any shape to our experience of him. Agnosis involves a perpetual to-ing and fro-ing between the two ways: knowing that we can say nothing; being convinced nonetheless that we must make the attempt; and realising finally (which returns us once again to our starting point) that these attempts, whatever they may bring of inspiration or insight, are still themselves partial and inadequate and need to be refined yet again in a revisiting of the silence of the divine darkness where our words and concepts fail us once more.

Thirdly, and finally before we can consider more positively what agnosis is and what it involves, there is one further set of ideas from which it needs to be clearly and firmly distinguished. Indeed, it is perhaps even more important that this should be done in this area than it is with regard to agnosticism and apophatic theology, since it concerns not a historical understanding of a word or a theological method, but the whole ambience of contemporary culture.

The culture of any age has a tendency to 'highjack' and overlay with its own meanings any concept whose definition is elastic enough to allow this to happen, and agnosis might easily therefore find itself given a secular baptism by a sceptical age. Agnosis therefore needs to be unambiguously dissociated from any decline into scepticism, relativism or any form of post-modern subjectivity or linguistically-defined outsidelessness. There is a crucial and very clear distinction to be drawn between unknowing – which is simply an acknowledgement of our inability or fundamental incapacity to know – and there being nothing to know. The fact that I cannot know something does not even remotely prejudice the existence or nature of that which I cannot know: my unknowing is a limitation of my own and places no corresponding limitations on that which is unknown. Unknowing does not in the least relativise the object of our unknowing, merely our perception and formulation of it, about whose own relativity we may be quite content.

On this account then, and this is precisely why the distinction we are drawing is so important, unknowing is perfectly compatible with the existence of a 'real' objective God: all we are saying when we admit our agnosis is that we cannot be certain, cognitively speaking, exactly who or what God is. Indeed we may go further than this and say, shocking though it may sound, that on a purely cognitive basis we cannot even be entirely certain that God exists. We may well find ourselves wanting to affirm his existence as something which we 'know' to be true, but properly speaking this certainty stems not from cognition but, as we shall argue later, from a very different kind of knowledge based on an equally different way of 'knowing'.

Thus far we have avoided a few pitfalls when speaking of agnosis, and have indicated that the term should never, as it were, be permitted to fall into the wrong company and be allowed to take on associations and nuances which are, in fact, completely alien to it. The second part of the task of this chapter, therefore, is to outline in more positive terms what agnosis is, what it involves, and how it will affect our approach to faith both in practical and in theological terms.

As was indicated in the introduction, the genesis of this book was a number of related ideas which lay behind A Space for Belief but which could not, largely for reasons of clarity and continuity of argument, be adequately explored there. At this point then, it is necessary to return to those ideas, and at the risk of slight repetition, to rehearse them again here in order to indicate the broad demands which agnosis makes upon our understanding of the Christian faith, so that these may then be spelled out in substantially more detail than was possible in A Space for Belief.

Agnosis makes demands both upon the individual's pattern of thinking and his or her response to the received content of faith, and also upon the church's corporate understanding of that faith with its accompanying corpus of doctrinal formulations and distinctions. As far as what might be called the 'structure of faith' is concerned, agnosis requires that we sit slightly looser to our doctrinal (and especially to our confessional)

frameworks than has, for the most part, traditionally been the case. There needs to be an awareness that although it may be the best that we can do (or at least the best that has yet been done), and although it may have been forged by some of the most brilliant and creative minds in successive ages, yet the whole framework is entirely provisional. It may, for most purposes, be adequate to shape our journey towards God, and it may very well feed us with sufficient glimpses of his/her love and majesty through our prayer and worship and service which are lived within that framework, yet with this must go the realisation that it is not in any sense definitive; that not only is there more of God than we have yet seen, but also that any human framework of ideas about God will never encapsulate or do justice to the reality of the God who is never reducible either to words or to concepts.

Again this may sound a frightening prospect to some, but it is not intended to suggest that our doctrinal framework needs to be dismantled completely or that Christianity should become somehow a 'contentless' faith. Agnosis does not involve any denial of the content of faith nor, as we have outlined above, any sort of disparaging or dismissive attitude towards those insights which have nurtured (and still do nurture) the faith of millions. It is simply that the framework, and our approach to it, needs to be loosened somewhat such that there is room for manoeuvre – and disagreement and debate – both within that framework itself, and in its relationship with other cultures and modes of knowledge including other religions. It is, as we have argued elsewhere, necessary that doctrine should provide – and be seen as providing – a space for belief rather than an interpretative fortress or prison. It should be, as Martin Henry aptly observes, that dogmas are 'rather like fences around the mysteries', and as he goes on to say that:

> They draw attention to where the mysteries lie but refuse ever to try to spell out their meaning definitively. In short, the church's dogmatic tradition is a tangible sign of how God is believed by Christian faith to lie beyond our comprehension.[1]

Here is a refreshing perception of doctrine indeed! Perhaps doctrine can continue to help us to breathe and not to stifle after all.

It is all very well to say this, but the central question is, how is it to be achieved? What does reaching this point involve? What attitudes or aspects of faith need to be reappraised in the light of agnosis if this understanding is to become a reality? In broad terms the answer to these questions is that there are two areas in particular which need to be re-examined. The first of these is our fundamental approach to the whole subject of the nature of God and the presuppositions which we bring both to our faith in general and specifically to our theology; and the second area is that of our response to what might be called some of the data and conceptual apparatus of our faith and especially the classical triad of scripture, tradition and reason.

First, then, we must explore our general approach to the realm of faith, theology and the nature and purposes of God. Christianity rejoices in being an historical faith, that is, not a collection merely of myths, legends and human ideas concerning divinity, but a faith which proclaims that God has revealed himself in history both in the Old Covenant and pre-eminently in the New Covenant through Jesus Christ. It is precisely here, however, that agnosis needs to begin to find a foothold. Tom Driver throws down the gauntlet in uncompromising fashion, and his warning is one which Christianity must heed time and again if it is not to over-reach itself:

> Those who are sure that they know what has happened in history, and what did not happen, are a menace to the Kingdom of God. They can be found among 'true believing' Christians as well as among secularists and atheists. The former insist upon the resurrection of Jesus as a historical 'fact' rather than a historical judgement made in the risk of faith. One of the risks of Christian faith is that one may be wrong about history.[2]

An historical faith is a challenging and a risky one, and without

being foolhardy we cannot claim certain objective knowledge even of the foundational events of that faith. What we have are not 'facts', as Driver points out, but an attitude towards history which is interpreted in the light of faith. Our interpretation of history may form or feed our faith, but our faith can never be used to try to 'prove' the accuracy of our history!

Similarly, we will need to approach the interpretation of that history with some caution, especially when it comes to trying to superimpose any metaphysical hermeneutical grid over history in order to explain not so much 'what' happened but 'how' or 'why' it happened. This caution might apply, for example, to such events as the Virgin Birth – or, more properly, of course, the Virginal Conception of Jesus – the resurrection, or our understanding of a particular miracle. Our attitude towards these things will need to be precisely that which is sketched so deftly by Michael Ramsey in the person of 'Mr B':

> I believe in a divine Christ, a Saviour who is indeed supernatural. And I am ready to believe that miraculous events happened in connection with the coming and the life of Christ. But looking at it honestly and cautiously, I cannot be quite sure what really happened in connection with his birth, because the narratives might be of a symbolic kind; and I cannot be quite sure what happened on Easter Day. For though I am quite sure that Jesus was and is alive, and though I am sure that something stupendous happened, I cannot with my historical conscience be really sure exactly what.[3]

Both in terms of 'what happened' and in our interpretation of what happened we must eschew certainty and embrace the more difficult and humbling task of unknowing – for in a curious way it is actually the 'easy option' to 'believe as many as six impossible things before breakfast'. It is much harder to discern and commit oneself to a faith to live for and, potentially, to die for, without the comforting illusion of chimerical 'certainty'. Without such 'certainty' – and if it is, as it must be, illusory, then

we are clearly better off without it – we may choose, guided no doubt by the wisdom of others and by the best evidence available to us, to believe in the historical veracity of this or that event, or to prefer one interpretation of a certain event over another. But we need to realise and to acknowledge both to ourselves and others that this is a matter of choice and not of orthodoxy and heresy, and with our choosing (whatever we may have decided, in the end, to choose) must go a salutary acceptance of the fact that we could be wrong.

It may be that for some we have gone far enough already, perhaps even too far, but in reality we must go further still. We may not proclaim certainty about the 'facts' of history, nor about our interpretation of those facts, and neither, even more momentously, may we claim certainty as to precisely what God has already done or may still be doing in and through that history and those 'facts'. Thus, to take an apposite example which has been discussed elsewhere in somewhat different terms, we are, properly speaking, unable to be too precise even about what God has 'done' through the death and resurrection of Jesus Christ – that complex of historical event and metaphysics which is referred to in doctrinal shorthand as the atonement.

In the course of a previous discussion of the atonement I have argued that we cannot put forward any one exclusive theory to account for the 'meaning' of it or to explain the 'mechanics' of what God has done through it. Here I would wish even to take this argument one step further, and to acknowledge that all the language which we use in connection with the atonement is figurative. Yes, we 'know that we have passed from death to life', but we cannot formulate with any precision what 'death' and 'life' mean in this context. Pre-critical Christianity might have been satisfied with the fires of hell on the one hand and eternal rest or some such conception on the other, but this will no longer do. We cannot be sure of precisely what it is that Christ's death and resurrection have redeemed us from, and we can no more give precise content to death or life, hell or heaven, than we can to the equally figurative ideas of 'up' and 'down' which we use to 'describe' their location.

Again it is important to stress that this does not prejudice the reality of those states of life and death, heaven and hell. It means only that we are unable to ascribe any too precise content to them: we do not know what exactly we are redeemed from; we only 'know', because we experience it, that we are redeemed into a renewed and more meaningful life and this, after all, is far more important. Similarly, we cannot know what we mean by 'heaven' or 'eternal life'; we can only trust that in some way which we cannot define our renewing and life-giving encounter with God will span the grave and that in the resurrection of Jesus – whatever form that exactly took – we shall find our own resurrection and eternal life, whatever (probably to our delighted surprise) that may turn out to mean.

We must therefore approach the whole historical and conceptual structure of our faith with respect but with a certain critical distance between us and it, expecting to find in it not a complete 'fast faith take-away' package of the nature, will and ways of God, but a series of pointers and signposts which may help to guide us on our way and may afford us glimpses of God, but which are not definitive and within which there is room for manoeuvre and for the co-existence of diverse opinions and experiences of the God who remains not only beyond our formulations but beyond our ken.

If our stance towards the entire conceptual framework of faith is as substantially governed by our unknowing as it appears it must be, then it is hardly surprising that the same is necessarily true of our outlook upon the primary 'data' and resources of our faith, namely scripture, tradition and reason. There is a great variety in the degree of hegemony accorded to scripture by the different denominations. Clearly if one belongs to a denomination which holds to the doctrine of the bible as being literally verbally inspired (i.e. that God 'told' the authors exactly what to write) then one will have severe difficulty in ever coming to terms with any suggestion of the need for agnosis in connection with scripture. For the rest of us, though, whilst the idea might sound a little more radical than we are perhaps

used to, there is no intrinsic barrier to the idea, especially if we can once accept that the concept of agnosis has itself, as we argued in chapters one and two, thoroughly scriptural roots.

To come to scripture through the way of unknowing means much more, though, than a simple uncertainty about particular matters of historical accuracy such as was discussed earlier in this chapter. It implies a profound unknowing towards the nature and purposes of God as they are revealed in scripture, but this is equally, because open, a deeply positive rather than negative approach to the bible. What is being eschewed through it is the kind of unbalanced or distorted vision of God which has so often in the history of the Christian church (and probably of all religions) been used to justify such-and-such a way of behaving, and which has often seemed to later generations to be a travesty of Christianity and a betrayal of the foundations of the gospel. It is all very well to say that the Israelites had a partial and lop-sided (or even thoroughly mistaken) idea of God when they slaughtered the inhabitants of the cities of Canaan in obedience to his 'command', but we need to be acutely aware that if we claim to 'know' too much then we run the grave risk of viewing scripture and therefore God in the light of our own purposes or desires, (much as we may say that the people of Israel did) such that we find there a God whom we have ourselves 'created' and superimposed upon the bible.

Indeed we need to come to scripture through the medium of what we might call a 'double agnosis': that is, conscious both of our own unknowing and that of the original authors of the biblical books. Our own unknowing has also to be read back into the pages of scripture. It is therefore not possible, from this point of view, to claim any sort of complete and infallible inspiration for scripture, and certainly not a divine literal verbal inspiration. Its authors may have been inspired in the sense that a poet or a composer may be said to be inspired, but they were not infallible, and neither were they merely the recipients of a pre-existing 'divine text'. Certainly much of the bible is gripping in its urgency and conviction, and its authors may have felt certain of

what they wrote (although as we have seen in chapters one and two, some of the biblical writers are certain only of human uncertainty!) but this in itself proves nothing about the adequacy of what they wrote to do justice to the God of whom they wrote.

Lest this should sound at all dismissive of scripture, it should be said that this is not, in any degree, the intention. All Christians would naturally and rightly wish to maintain that there is real inspiration and truth contained in scripture since it has empowered and nourished successive generations of Christians. With all of this I would readily concur, but the point at issue is that even this living experience of the bible should not blind us to its intrinsic uncertainty and unknowing – otherwise we are in danger of imprisoning God in the pages of the bible. God is 'more' than any witness to him, even the bible, and even when the bible appears to us to be most profound or most inspiring we need still – and perhaps especially – to remember that a double agnosis is at work, and that both the text itself and our interpretation of it are, by definition, inadequate for the reality of the God with whom they have to do.

If this is true of scripture, it is even more true with regard to tradition, which though it may be clad in the venerability of age is not to the same extent hedged around with the supposed taboos of sacredness. Every church, needless to say, has its 'tradition' and, within that, its traditions. This may be very obvious in the case of the older established churches or of those which overtly place great store by their particular 'tradition'. It may equally be much less obvious on the part of 'newer' churches, or of those which affect to be unbound by tradition and to rely on the present day leading of the Holy Spirit. However, even these churches rapidly develop a tradition, even if this is unacknowledged; for it is actually just as much a tradition to say, 'This church believes in this or that activity of the Holy Spirit or conducts its services in such-and-such an informal fashion' as it is to look back to the *Book of Common Prayer*, or the Council of Trent or even the Council of Nicea for pointers to one's ecclesial identity. Like it or not, any church which remains in existence over a

reasonable period of time will have a tradition, whether acknowledged or unacknowledged, written or unwritten, spoken
or unspoken.

These traditions will also, of course, vary substantially, and
as we have argued will be accorded a different weight depending upon the value which each church places upon its tradition.
In certain denominations, therefore, tradition has come to be
valued very highly indeed. Similarly, tradition concerns a wide
variety of issues affecting doctrine, church government, liturgical practice, ethics and so on. In all of these areas tradition may
be inexpressibly helpful in contributing to the opinions and
practices of the present day, but agnosis again requires that it
should not – indeed cannot – be seen as definitive or absolute.

I have no intention, in any part of this discussion, to give offence either to my own Anglican Communion or to any other
church community, and even less to indulge in any 'point scor-
ing' between churches. Thus the following remarks refer to the
Roman Catholic Church simply because theirs is the most clearly
and 'officially' sanctioned position, but it is one which many
other churches might well claim for their own practices and
opinions – although of course they would also throw up their
hands in righteous indignation were one ever to suggest that
their attitude was anything like that of the Church of Rome! Be
that as it may, agnosis is fundamentally incompatible with the
notion that any church or individual can proclaim their 'infallibility' with regard to any element of their teaching tradition. To
those who do not hold such a position it is – and I can only apol-
ogise for the inevitable offence – not so much the arrogance as
the folly of it which is so hard to credit. The basic problem with
the argument for papal infallibility – and therefore with the infallibility of any other church or leader, in whatever very different terms they may choose to express it – is its perfect circularity.
How do you know that the pope or the church is infallible?
Because he/it cannot err. How do you know that they cannot
err? Because they are infallible. It is, indeed, as circular as the
equally improbable – but more widely discredited – argument

for the infallibility of scripture which I have discussed at some length elsewhere.[4]

What will be, of course, particularly interesting, is when one pope (and it is almost bound to happen sooner or later) feels bound to call into question (infallibly, of course) the infallibility of a previous pope. At this point the question of agnosis surfaces definitively and potentially very uncomfortably *viv-à-vis* the entire tradition.

However, the issue is much wider than this, for many denominations, as we have argued, accord a kind of unwritten and unspoken informal infallibility to their tradition and agnosis radically calls this into question also. No tradition, however august, can bear the weight of infallibility and certainty being placed upon it. And again, as with scripture, we are in the presence of a double agnosis: either tradition itself may be misguided at points, or our interpretation and application of it may be awry – or even, potentially, both.

Just as with scripture, then, the potential – indeed the requirement – for agnosis is present in our engagement with our tradition. Valuable and aesthetically pleasing though it may be, tradition is not so much a steel rod as an elastic band connecting past and present, and our own unknowing requires us to be equally flexible in our interpretation and use of it. There needs to be room within the broad outlines of any tradition for differing interpretations even of fundamental doctrinal points, and there must certainly be even more room for debate (and humility) about entirely secondary issues of church order and government and other 'extra-biblical' areas of discussion.

In coming to both scripture and tradition in a spirit of unknowing, both as far as the 'data' and our interpretation of it is concerned, we have already begun to look with unknowing on the third member of the triad – reason. And as we apply the idea of agnosis to our own use of reason an enthralling and never-ending circle is created in the making of which scripture and tradition are yet and ever again consulted and questioned. Thus we come to scripture and tradition aware of our own agnosis and therefore of the limits of our own reason, and at the same time aware also that these same limitations apply to the biblical authors and to all the minds – even those of the greatest and most inspiring figures – in the tradition of the church. Yet we know that out of this interchange, with all of its unknowing, a space for belief and inspiration along our pilgrimage of faith must be found – all that we find being still, however, provisional. The whole process is a never ending cycle of passionate conviction indissolubly wedded to radical unknowing which crisscrosses back and forth through the centuries, and finds in each generation its perhaps bewildering but nonetheless life-giving locus in the present.

In the course of this chapter, then, in terms both of general attitudes and our approach to some of the specific resources and data of our faith, we have explored at least some of the elements involved in a genuine contemporary agnosis, and discovered that it will mean a good deal of letting-go. It is now important, therefore, to turn to the question of why it is that this letting-go and embracing of agnosis is so important. As we do this we shall hopefully glimpse the fact that to let go is, potentially, to be blessed, and we will perceive ourselves in the light of the biblical truth that to do what looks like losing our life is, in reality, to find it anew.

# CHAPTER 5

## *The Importance of Agnosis Today*

We have now reached a point where we have seen that agnosis, although it might seem initially a threatening idea if we are encountering it for the first time, is actually deeply biblical and also firmly rooted in the history of the church, and furthermore that it is also, if radical, in essence a deeply simple, if yet profound, concept. So much so, indeed, that one might be inclined to ask why, if it is so straightforward an idea, are we concerned to go to such lengths to explore its origins and stress its importance? Does something which is so uncomplicated and self-evident really need such treatment? I readily confess to having a certain amount of sympathy with such an attitude, but the problem is that agnosis is only 'obvious' once we have been made aware of it. It is simple in the same way that riding a bicycle is simple once you can do it. It is, if you like, only self-evident in the way that the wheel became self-evident once some megalithic genius had had the inspiration to invent it – prior to that it had plainly not been self-evident at all. So too with agnosis: it is obvious that our 'knowing' has limits, but we are so used to living in a world of knowledge that it is all too easy to forget this reality, and therefore, unlike the wheel which remains self-evident, agnosis is a concept which seems to need to be rediscovered time and time again.

The reasons for this need for continual rediscovery of the way of unknowing are themselves a prime instance of why agnosis is – and will always remain – so vitally important. To say that we live in a world which puts a premium on knowledge is an understatement. Not only is knowledge accorded tremendous prestige – witnessed to by the ever increasing competition for places at third level education as more and more people attempt to gain the qualifications which are seen as essential for 'success' – but knowledge in almost every field is accumulating in an almost geometrical progression with every passing lifetime.

It is probably true that with the possible exception of certain periods of relative stagnation this has happened in most ages, but certainly the twentieth and twenty-first centuries are the ones in which it may be seen – and by the so-called 'older generation' has also been experienced – most dramatically. In only a little over one hundred years we have moved from horses to space exploration, from rifles to atomic missiles, from gas to electricity to email and beyond! I am sure that the feeling has been the same for previous generations as a new world has succeeded the old one in the course of their own lifetime, but it is hard to feel their discomfiture at the rate of change as keenly, and as personally, as we feel our own. Thus, to cite a minor example, I am sure that it will only be a couple of years before my elder son, who is at present twelve years old, comes home from school telling me that my word processor is out of date – which it undoubtedly is! – and asking why Daddy isn't using Windows XP Professional (or whatever else may represent the state of the art by then) like any sensible and 'with it' twelve year old.

Unless this new knowledge can be responded to coherently and rapidly – and this is clearly a task which needs to be done again and again – Christianity is at risk of being placed under severe strain. That this can happen is due to the apparently 'timeless' nature of the central Christian message allied to the necessarily contextual – and to use the word of the moment, enculturated – 'dress' in which it is presented. Thus depending on the exact nature of the concepts and general culture in which it is clothed, the message of Christianity can appear to have been left behind by the progress of other ideas. A message which is itself timeless becomes imprisoned in the dress of an outdated world view, and so appears, from the perspective of a new worldview to have nothing left to offer.

This has happened too often, too obviously, and too painfully for us to need to rehearse any of the grisly details of specific occasions here: Christian history is littered with the debris of inadequate responses to the questions posed by the contemporary world. What is interesting to note, however, is the corollary between this process and the present day decline in church membership in the west, which, whatever ingenious 'spin' may be put on the statistics by each denomination, seems nonetheless to be a reality. This decline almost certainly reflects 'popular opinion' about the relationship between the world of faith and the 'everyday' scientific world – a popular opinion which is pseudo-scientific rather than genuinely scientifically informed and which is, typically, somewhere around a whole generation out of date as far as its understanding of contemporary science is concerned.

Thus, as we have observed elsewhere, God and the categories of faith were largely dismissed by science, philosophy and linguistic theory in its widest sense during the middle years of the twentieth century, perhaps until as recently as the early to mid-1980s, when the phenomena of post-modernism and deconstruction first came to be seriously questioned, independently but almost simultaneously, by scientists, philosophers and theologians. As one might expect, each 'round' of this debate took a generation or so to 'filter down', and popular culture is now therefore infected with a rash of notions about the irrelevance of God to the 'real' world which is governed by scientific laws and so on; and all this at precisely the same moment as the academic and intellectual world has rehabilitated God as an entity seriously to be reckoned with. It will be interesting to see whether the churches report a rise in churchgoing in twenty or twenty five years' time as these ideas in their turn take a hold on popular culture.

Whether this happens or not, though, may well depend on the quality of the church's response – and not just that of theologians – to the present decline, and the problem is that this response can easily be, and has on more than one occasion proved to be, counterproductive. When troubles threaten we have a natural human instinct to be conservative and defensive, determined to protect and preserve what we have. This may be laudable, but in the realm of faith it can also be disastrous. Thus our response to a decline in numbers and to a widespread sense of the 'outdatedness' and irrelevance of Christianity is to take refuge in 'certainty'. The trouble is that this certainty tends to be precisely over those things which have most recently been radically called into question, and it turns out to be a certainty which is so spurious as to prove that if this is what Christianity really is, then it does indeed have nothing to offer – except perhaps the ostrich's hole in the sand which will at least enable it to remain oblivious while the rest of it is blown to smithereens by the culture around it.

In these conditions, which are ones which pertain to a greater or lesser degree in every age, and which are certainly powerfully in evidence in the present day, agnosis is at once a practical and a deeply spiritual response. Both of these aspects will be drawn upon throughout the remainder of this study, and we will confine ourselves here, therefore, to the briefest sketch.

It is practical in that it represents an honest and credible as well as open and flexible approach to changing circumstances and knowledge. It allows the church freely to acknowledge that it does not know with certainty how various things fit together or how, for example, humanity and divinity, or the natural and the miraculous, are precisely related. Similarly, the church does not have to pretend that it has an exhaustive blueprint of God's nature which then has to be matched with increasing inaccuracy (rather like pre-Copernican attempts to keep the earth at the centre of things) to whatever the current state of knowledge may be. In a condition of faithful agnosis the church and its theology are enabled to work alongside, rather than against, new developments in human knowledge as they attempt to discern God's will and purposes unfolding in many new ways through those developments.

But it is not enough for the church to be merely practical:

faithfulness to her calling demands that her life is one which has a primary spiritual orientation, and here too agnosis enables the church's response to the world to be at least as much spiritual as practical. That this is so is a result of the same qualities of flexibility and openness which enable the response to be practical: in this instance practicality and spirituality actually go hand-in-hand. Agnosis thus allows for (and indeed requires) precisely the sort of open and flexible response to God which is not immediately threatened by the latest new discovery or theory. God is not forced into becoming anything approaching a 'God of the gaps' who is threatened with being finally squeezed out as the gaps become smaller and smaller. On the contrary, agnosis is content (for God's sake, as it were, as well as the church's) to acknowledge that we do not at present 'know' – and maybe will not know for a very long time, or indeed will perhaps never in this life know – how God relates to this or that aspect of his creation whose secrets we are continually discovering. We are well able to live with a degree – quite probably even a large degree – of unknowing since, in allowing faith to co-exist in an atmosphere of mutual seeking alongside other disciplines and cultural traditions, it allows us also the space and the freedom to proclaim from an experiential standpoint (which is an equally important category of knowledge) God's presence and activity even if we may not always locate or describe these with absolute conceptual precision.

All of the foregoing represents a broad indication of why agnosis constitutes an important part of the church's response both to God and to the opinions and findings of other disciplines which impinge on our understanding of God and of his activity, and we must now therefore explore a number of more specific reasons why agnosis is so important for the church today and why it is, properly, fundamental to the nature of faith and therefore also of theology.

First of all, then, there is a central crucial issue at stake *vis-à-vis* the nature and activity of God himself which raises the question both of the appropriateness of any particular way of 'con-

ceptualising' God and the consequent danger of falling almost
unconsciously into idolatry, and also of our response to and co-
operation with God's will and activity. It is, furthermore, an
issue which is particularly germane to Christianity as an incarnational faith and suggests in what might seem a paradoxical
fashion that the 'closer' God's approach to us becomes, the more
it behoves us to respond with humble agnosis rather than with
anything apparently more 'concrete' but probably therefore also
more exclusive or arrogant. Timothy Kinahan puts this potentially bewildering aspect of incarnation most beautifully when
he writes:

> Incarnation, personhood, was needed more adequately to re-
> veal the nature of the living, communicating God, with all
> the dangers that that entailed. Somehow God decided that it
> wasn't enough for humanity to get all steamed up about
> words. They needed something really confusing – a person
> who defied all previous, and all logical, categories.[1]

Our faith then, is firmly incarnational both in the primary sense
of hinging on the incarnation of God in Christ, and in the secondary and derivative sense of believing that this mode of activity is characteristic of God. God, we believe, is a God who works
in and through humanity which, in both its primary and secondary senses, involves a large measure of openness and unknowing on our part. Primarily we believe that God, in Jesus
Christ, took human nature to himself, but all of our deepest
metaphysical explorations of 'how' this might be possible are
only pictorial and symbolic attempts to give us even the beginnings of a glimmering as to what this might mean. We certainly
have no exact or exhaustive explanation of the 'mechanics' of
incarnation. Likewise, as we have argued previously, neither do
we have any certain knowledge of the nature of the redemption
wrought in the incarnation, except in so far as we experience
ourselves to be redeemed and renewed. All we can 'know' is the
process of redemption *in via* rather than its genesis or its ultimate destination.

If this is true of God's primary incarnational work of re-demption in Jesus Christ it is equally – though no doubt in a dif-ferent fashion – true of his secondary mode of incarnational ac-tivity through his continuing involvement with, and activity in human lives. Again we may very well feel experientially 'sure' of God's activity through the medium of human life, especially if we have witnessed it powerfully for ourselves through the ministry of another person which has facilitated our own en-counter with God, but at the same time we can no more pin down the 'how' of this activity or predict its presence through the application of known 'factors' than we can fully account for God's presence in Jesus Christ. We may experience its effects, but we cannot say precisely what it 'means' to be indwelt by the Holy Spirit, nor account accurately for the exact manner in which God is present with his people in worship or in the an-swering of prayer. We may feel these things to be so to the depths of our being, but we cannot adequately give reason for how it is that they come to be so.

At these points agnosis is of immeasurable importance, both for its own sake, because it most truly reflects the inadequacy of our human knowledge, and also because of the relationship be-tween our 'knowledge' (or otherwise) of God's nature and activ-ity and the actual exercise of that nature and activity on the part of a God who has revealed himself in such thoroughgoing incarnational terms.

The point at stake here is a somewhat complex and – it must be admitted – a somewhat speculative one, but it deserves care-ful consideration both in the light of the incarnational teaching of our faith and in the light of our own experience of God as in-carnational. Incarnation, then, involves in some form or another, a self-limitation on the part of God, and this applies to incarn-ation both in its primary and secondary senses. In terms of the incarnation of Jesus Christ it is obvious that this is so. One may or may not agree with the 'modernist' view of Charles Gore and his contemporaries about the details of kenotic theory, and in-deed I would prefer the phrase 'self-limitation' to 'self-emptying', but it is reasonable to assume that for God to become human there is a substantial degree of self-limitation involved unless the incarnation is to be so docetic as to be, effectively, as the Cappadocian Fathers realised, meaningless.

By extension and derivation, therefore, it may equally be assumed that God's continuing involvement not merely with but in and through the medium of human lives necessitates a still greater degree of divine self-limitation. Essentially this entails the assumption – admittedly unsubstantiated, but in keeping with what we believe of God's incarnational and broadly kenotic nature as revealed in Jesus Christ – that God will not do, through human agency, that which human nature is not capable in itself of bearing or, in however faltering a fashion, of providing the means for accomplishing.

Admittedly there is a complicating factor at work here, although this should naturally add to rather than detract from the quality of our agnosis. This complicating factor is simply (!) that we do not know precisely what it means to be fully human or what that full humanity is capable of bearing or accomplishing. All that we know of humanity is our present experience of it, and we therefore do not know what the capabilities of a 'perfect' or completely fulfilled human nature might be, or how close to the emulation of divinity it might thereby become. Thus, profoundly, we cannot know for certain what God is capable of doing, without violating human nature (as we believe he will not) through that human nature. Here, also, ought incidentally to be the final refutation of any charge that agnosis is reductive or negative in its implications: we may well, if we allow ourselves the dangerous freedom to come under its influence, be open to more, not less, from God.

This depth of agnosis, however, puts no limits on God, except those of his own self-limitation, and so we should merely be open enough to expect surprises from God[2] – again entirely consistent with our unknowing. What might put limits upon God, though, may well be an over-confident and un-agnostic 'certainty' about the ways in which God acts in human life. If we limit our own conception of human nature such that we live within a constricted humanity of our own devising, certain that this is 'really' what it means to be human, then might it not be that God will not violate our vision of ourselves and therefore is no longer free to act in certain ways in which he might otherwise act? It may be that God's self-limitation is so radical that we have been given the 'power' to limit God: if we will not see the possibility of his action because we are 'sure' that he only works in this or that fashion, then it is possible that God cannot act if he is to remain true to his fundamentally incarnational nature.

If this sounds a little over-speculative or far-fetched, we might make a useful comparison with God's action in Jesus Christ. A crucial question is: do we believe Jesus' humanity to be full enough that he could have said 'No' to God? I think we must do so; and if we do, then we have logically to accept the possibility that God, if Jesus' free will (and his own self-limitation, and therefore the probity of the incarnation) were to be preserved, would have had to accept this 'No' and witness the failure of incarnation and redemption in Jesus Christ. Shocking perhaps, but possible unless we embrace a docetic Christ; and if God could potentially be constrained by the humanity of Jesus, then it is less unreasonable to suppose that his actions may likewise be modified (or even prevented) by the constraints of freedom which our 'certainty' or agnosis allows. Maybe, if we 'know' who God is and what he does then this will indeed be the limit of his activity: if we do not know, God may be free to be truly himself.

This first reason for the prime importance of agnosis, then, is concerned with the realisation of God's own self-identity, subject, of course, only to his own self-limitation (the extent of which is unknown to us) in his dealings with humanity. In a complementary fashion, the other reasons which we will adduce here are all related to our own identity, especially insofar as that is, as created beings, governed by our relationship with God.

This relationship, though, has a tendency to be misrepresented in one of two ways, either of which destroys what is, I believe, a delicate balance implicit in the relationship between God and ourselves. Briefly, the first form of misrepresentation stems from an over emphasis on the 'dependency' or 'servant-like' nature of the relationship, and the second springs, in reaction to this, from an arrogant overthrowing of all traces of inequality in the relationship.

It is possible, then – although, as will become clear, I believe inaccurate – to portray the relationship between ourselves and God as being wholly one of 'obedience', 'dependence' and 'inferiority'. This may stem from any number of sources: whether a misunderstanding of the nature of dependence, and with it Schliermacher's resoundingly influential 'feeling of absolute dependence', or an equally naïve misreading of the familiar terms of creator and creature which all too easily threaten to exalt the creator at the expense of the creature. Yes, we are creatures and we are dependent, but this is not the whole story. It is a part of the story and one which may quickly be magnified out of all proportion.

When this happens the result is a depressingly familiar caricature of Christianity such as has been rightly ridiculed by a number (amongst others) of the *Sea of Faith* theologians; and whilst not everyone would share their basic theological principles, their criticisms of what is perceived all too often as 'the Christian life' (and unfortunately by those outside it as much as by those within, which must do wonders for Christian witness!) remain valid.

The main thrust of these criticisms is that Christianity has within it the seeds, which are then frequently nurtured, whether consciously or unconsciously, by the church, of what has been termed a 'slave-mentality' – a criticism which goes back at least as far as Nietzsche. By this is meant the fact that, depending on how it is presented, the Christian faith may readily come to be perceived (and often is so perceived) as involving a framework of rules which we are expected to keep, and as being more concerned with the 'negative goodness' of avoiding sin than with anything more positive. Similarly, its 'aim' is equally submissive: the believer seeks his or her salvation, the way to which is through obedience and quiescence. Certainly this is a travesty of a vibrant living Christianity – but look at all too many churches.

Such a 'slave-mentality' might even have been, if not appropriate, at least generally acceptable in previous eras, as for example in the world of Cranmer's Prayer Book where dependence and obedience and 'knowing one's station' was the lot of the vast majority of people. A similar approach in religious matters would not have seemed at all out of place in a world such as this. Indeed, the fact that this worldview survived – in the church at least – until something like the middle of the nineteenth century is attested to by a verse (now excised) from Mrs Alexander's famous hymn *All things bright and beautiful*, which runs:

> The rich man in his castle,
> The poor man at his gate;
> God made them high and lowly,
> And ordered their estate.

However, although the intervening centuries have pruned away a good deal of the excessive concern with human depravity and sinfulness exhibited in the *Book of Common Prayer*, the underlying conception of faith has remained largely constant, being expressed now in the collects in frequently repeated petitions to 'keep us faithful' and 'help us to follow' in this or that respect. The pattern is the same, if less crudely drawn: all we can do is live a 'secondary' life in obedient response to God's known will and commands.

It is, in large measure, this sense of Christianity being a closed system within the neat boundaries of which God's will is 'known' which creates (or at least exacerbates) the problem. Agnosis undercuts the closedness of the system, and thereby enables us to move away from the accompanying mentality. For we do not know with any certainty what God's will may be in a thousand-and-one new and specific situations, and our role is far more substantial than blindly to obey a set of rules and avoid sin.

There are hints, even in scripture, that humanity is to enter into a creative partnership with God, and this is very much the possibility which agnosis opens up. Certainly we are created: but by the very fact of our unknowing we are created to be creative. In a curious way it is precisely our condition of unknowing which dictates that this should be so. For unknowing itself demands that we seek to know more, and for the most part the human race appears to be filled with a kind of 'divine discontent' which propels it ever onward towards the acquisition of knowledge and skills. This is very obviously so in the case of what might be called straightforward human knowledge and achievement, hence the continual attempts to discover more about the creation, to invent new technologies, or to do something – be it run one hundred metres or compose a symphony – better than it has yet been done. It is so too, although inevitably less overtly, in the realm of faith, and indeed in ways which are sometimes linked to discoveries and inventions in other areas. Thus, both in prayer and in theology, Christians are continually reflecting on their faith and attempting to articulate their experience and understanding of God more clearly, and also endeavouring to discern what the will of God might be in a myriad new situations, as for example, in the ever-developing flux of medical and genetic ethics.

Our life of faith is thus shaped by our unknowing into being a creative venture in partnership with God, as we seek always to learn more of ourselves and of the world, to discern God's unfolding will and activity in the new and unfamiliar, and to grow through our openness and unknowing into an ever-increasing faith and trust in the God whom we experience so profoundly but will only ever understand inadequately. We will, incidentally, return more fully to consider in greater detail what our whole conception of faith looks like in the light of agnosis in a later chapter.

In this vision of faith we are not just 'keeping the rules'. We are licensed to take risks and to get things wrong sometimes. We are constrained neither by fear nor by false limits which we place upon God: on the contrary, we are open to every manifestation of God's incessant and yet often surprising grace, and even more importantly we are set free to love without limits, confident, as I have argued elsewhere, that errors made in good faith and in the service of love will be more readily forgiven than an unbending, uncreative and loveless obedience to 'duty'.

If agnosis delivers us from a bondage of false certainty and fear of failure, it also quite plainly avoids the other extreme – to a large extent well represented by the *Sea of Faith* theologians mentioned earlier, although it is an attitude by no means confined to them, of asserting human autonomy and exalting it to such a pitch that humanity assumes the attributes and functions of divinity and God is no longer required, except perhaps as a word or a set of – now entirely human – externalised ideals.

Whether or not one agrees with this estimate of God (and, as may have become evident already, I personally do not), is obviously a factor in one's analysis of the importance of unknowing, but it is by no means the only one. If one feels that such an approach to theology is fundamentally misguided, then agnosis clearly has a function. The *Sea of Faith* school of thought may well be right to reject the 'smallness' and 'rule-boundness' of the faith and the God which they have inherited, but in so doing they have ironically fallen into a different version of the same trap from which they have wished so vehemently and striven so hard to escape.

Their attitude is, if not exactly arrogant, at least overconfident, and in fleeing from false certainties about God which constrict him (and us) they have landed in a set of different but equally false presuppositions about God's non-existence and the capabilities of human nature. Agnosis suggests that we can no more be 'certain' of God's non-existence (or his existence as an 'ideal') than we can be about the precise details of any more 'real' existence which may be ascribed to him. Even from a perspective of total sympathy with the *Sea of Faith* approach, it might still be argued that claiming complete autonomy and 'control' for humanity is over-stepping the mark, and that whether or not one conceives God as really existing there is nonetheless plenty more about even our human life which we might do well to be more agnostic about. As for God, it is hard to see how he can reasonably be dismissed on grounds of 'knowledge' any more than he can be fully accounted for on those same grounds.

Even if one accepts the *Sea of Faith* estimate of God, then, there still remains a valid place for agnosis solely in connection with the limitations and provisionality of our human knowledge; but if one disagrees with that estimate then agnosis has a major role to play in articulating the reasons for that disagreement. These reasons are both intellectual, in connection with our being unable to 'know' of God's non-existence as outlined above, and springing from this also relational, as establishing our identity and a right relationship with God (who, from this perspective, is viewed as real); that is, our life is lived, both as a part of the natural order and in relationship with God, constantly in the light of our own awareness of our limitations and lack of omniscience. Agnosis emphatically does not lead us to fall back once more into slavery, but it does at least engender a touch of humility as far as our own capabilities are concerned, and this remains important whatever answer one gives to the prior question of God's existence.

Both God's identity and freedom and our identity and freedom in relationship with him are fostered by an acknowledgement of unknowing, and finally our joyous response to that identity and relationship with God (and just to the amazingness of the gift of life) is also nurtured by agnosis. For agnosis is consistent with (and may well call forth) a sense – which the rather fact-laden and prosaic twentieth and twenty-first centuries have often forgotten – of profound wonder and of a sense of awe at the mystery of our existence. Michael Mayne's delightful book *This Sunrise of Wonder* captures this sense perfectly, and quoting G. K. Chesterton he writes:

> At the back of our brains, so to speak, there is a forgotten blaze or burst of astonishment at our own existence. The ob-

ject of the artistic and spiritual life is to dig for this sunrise of wonder.[3]

Neither is this sense of wonder and mystery one which will ever diminish even if our knowledge should increase, for as Michael Mayne comments:

A mystery in the religious, as opposed to the P. D. James sense, is not some truth that can be fully understood once the wit and cunning of our brains have fathomed it out. It is implicit in life itself, and above all in the mystery that is me. 'Mysteries', it has been said, 'are not truths that lie beyond us; they are truths that comprehend us.' But which we do not comprehend.[4]

Agnosis is receptive to this attitude of wonder and mystery – and of joy in it, and both our daily living and specifically our relationship with God will be enriched far more by embracing our unknowing than they will by living hedged in by pseudo-certainties which, whilst they may sometimes feel familiar and comfortable, nonetheless narrow our horizons and limit our vision.

Agnosis, then, is as significant in the religious life as it has always been – perhaps in view of the remarks made at the beginning of this chapter, more so – and it offers a life-enhancing freedom from a variety of somewhat limited (and limiting) positions. More than this, though, it offers a number of major and very specific positive elements to our understanding of Christianity and to the credibility of our witness to it, and having considered some of the problems from which agnosis may help to deliver us, we may now hope to establish more fully where it is that, if followed, it may (hopefully rejoicing) lead us.

# CHAPTER 6

# From Literalism to Liberation

In the previous chapter we explored some of the various pitfalls into which theology may wander and argued that a healthy (and honest) dose of unknowing may help to save us from many of these. As we now move to begin to consider the positive benefits of agnosis there will inevitably be some measure of overlap, not so much in precise content as in method, although the emphasis will be different.

Thus in the preceding chapter we have considered agnosis largely in its, as it were, redemptive capacity; here, and in the succeeding chapters, we shall be looking at least as much at the gains which it brings as at the problems from which it delivers us. The overlap, however, exists in the fact that any potential benefit has an equal dark side which will surface if the benefit is not embraced, and thus therefore there will still be a sense involved of moving from one negative state to another more positive one. The essential difference, however, is that cumulatively in providing these positive directions, agnosis can not only enable us to avoid a number of problems but also helps to shape, profoundly and fundamentally the whole life and pattern of the church and of the theology on which it feeds.

We have alluded already to the fact that although agnosis has always been in an underlying way an essential ingredient of the Christian faith, if not always being accorded due recognition. Indeed its potential significance today is perhaps greater than it has been at any stage in the church's long history. That this is so is due to a number of particular issues of contemporary significance which will be addressed in this and the following chapters. Of these, the first, and almost certainly the most immediately threatening, is the spectre of fundamentalism.

The first matter which must be addressed is that of what precisely is meant in this discussion by the much used (and abused) term 'fundamentalism'. One could adduce various dictionary definitions which indicate the precise origins of the word in early twentieth-century America, and which outline what are, strictly speaking, according to these origins, the proper boundaries of the term. What is meant here – and very often in other discussions, other than ones referring directly to these origins – is something somewhat wider although still clearly defined. It is a complex of ideas and attitudes which stem from the basic fundamentalist premises about the inspiration, inerrancy and literal interpretation of scripture, but which then applies these same rigid standards to a whole gamut of interrelated topics and areas. And curiously, somewhere along the way, the original scriptural dimension can, at times, be lost. Thus one may be, for example, what we will later define as being a social and cultural fundamentalist without necessarily being a biblical fundamentalist at all – or only so in part. It is this spread of the mind-set of fundamentalism into other areas which distinguishes fundamentalism as it is examined here from what might be called the classical fundamentalist standpoint which always retains its origins in scripture.

There is one further point to be clarified before we can proceed any further with a detailed exposition of the issue of fundamentalism and the response of agnosis. This is that although fundamentalism has arisen in some form or another in almost every age (but has, of course, not been known by this precise term until the last century), it has probably never posed so direct a threat to the well-being of Christianity as it does today. Thus it is one thing to insist on the literal interpretation of scripture in a pre-critical age, when admittedly others may be advocating its figurative or metaphorical interpretation; it is quite another to be similarly insistent in an age in which not only Christianity but every other realm of thought is required to be perpetually reflexively self-critical in order to have any credibility whatsoever. Quite simply, if fundamentalism wins the day in the present climate, Christianity, although it may witness a temporary increase in numbers, is assured of nothing less (or more) than existence in a ghetto whose margins will be eroded and whose citadels defeated as surely as those of Ptolomaic astronomy were by the observations of Copernicus or those of Newtonian physics by the theories and discoveries of Einstein.

However, the difficulty is compounded by the fact that it is exactly in those conditions in which fundamentalism is likely to be most disastrous that it is also most likely, ironically, to flourish. Thus the reason why Christianity needs to be self-aware and self-critical and to avoid fundamentalism at all costs is that we live in an age which demands this sort of reflexive self-criticism in every other area of life. This tends, however, to breed an underlying current of scepticism and rationalism, and it is in response to this religiously corrosive atmosphere that fundamentalism is most likely to arise.

The truth of this would appear to be borne out by the fact – which is much more than merely a coincidence – that it is not only within Christianity that fundamentalism is currently on the increase. Thus the Islamic world is experiencing the same phenomenon and one would hazard a guess that it is probably for much the same reasons. The realm of faith has come under a certain amount of pressure from an increasingly sceptical world, and one response to this is to retreat into one's scriptural and doctrinal fortress and man the barricades to keep the intruders out. This may be a response which is borne of insecurity and fear, but this makes it more, rather than less, common.

Today's intellectual and social climate, then, is a propitious one for fundamentalism. We have mentioned the fact that a fundamentalist mind-set manifests itself in a number of settings in addition to the original application of the term in relation to scripture, and it is these other flowerings of fundamentalism which are of most interest to us here, especially with regard to the way in which they can continue to flourish even when severed from any integral scriptural point of reference.

Genuine scriptural fundamentalism has a well-documented

identity and history, and need concern us here only briefly in two particular respects, both of which indicate that the basic premises of fundamentalism are unsound, and that our response to scripture needs to be far more interrogative and 'involved' than fundamentalism will allow it to be.

First, then, the bible itself displays a marked resistance to any sort of over-literal interpretation. Quite apart from the fact that it is shot through with unknowing, it is also full of pictures, images and stories which demand to be interpreted symbolically or metaphorically rather than literally. Read as history, the story of Jonah – apart from being more than slightly unlikely! – is no more than one reluctant prophet's experience; read as myth it is a profound exploration of a number of aspects of our relationship with and response to God. Similarly, the bible, being a collection of books, displays a rich variety of ideas and concepts which are not easily reconciled with one another if we insist on interpreting it literally. Furthermore, there are many self-contradictions both between different books and even within individual books, as well as lacunae which literalism cannot bridge. Which account of the creation is the 'right' one and what do we then do with the other one? Where on earth (the phrase seems appropriate!) did Cain's wife materialise from?

Secondly, not only is the bible resistant to fundamentalism, but the whole notion of biblical inerrancy and verbal inspiration is potentially – and that potential will always be realised – self-defeating. In theory it is possible to hold such a notion, but in practice it is actually impossible to do so consistently, and once any inconsistency creeps in the theory is dead. Thus if the bible is inerrant and verbally inspired we have no possible excuse for omitting any part of it. We should, therefore, in theory still be stoning homosexuals and adulterers, for example. In practice, however, we believe this to be wrong (and not merely politically incorrect) and so we do not do it. Scripture is thereby 'judged' and found to be in error on this particular point; and if here, why not elsewhere. Once the process has been begun there is no going back: without complete logical inconsistency we cannot any longer argue for the inerrancy of scripture, for there is no possible reason why it should be inerrant at all points except this one … and this one … and this one …

As we have observed, however, even the complete destruction of any reasonable case for biblical fundamentalism does not prevent a similar kind of mind-set from operating in other spheres relating to the religious life. These spheres may conveniently be delineated (in order as they move away from scripture as a basis) as being doctrinal, ethical and socio-cultural. Strictly speaking, as we have acknowledged, the term 'fundamentalism' is not entirely accurate when applied in these contexts, and the broader term of 'literalism' which we have adopted for the title of this chapter is more appropriate, although it remains true that there is a family resemblance of attitude between these other spheres and the world of scriptural fundamentalism.

The common thread which stems from biblical fundamentalism and encompasses all other varieties of literalism is that of a set of clearly defined boundaries and rules together with an accompanying certainty that these are the 'right' ones – both the rules and the certainty having their ultimate origins in, but not necessarily any longer entirely depending upon, scripture.

Closest to scripture, then, is what we might call doctrinal literalism. This is a complex of ideas which adds up to a fully worked-out schema of creation, fall, redemption and eschatology. This schema and the response which it demands from its adherents is distinguished by three features in particular.

First, the Christian faith is construed as a complete and definitive package of beliefs which must be accepted *en bloc*. There is no room for a sense of discovery and creativity in faith such as we have argued for here, and the reason why there is no room for it is that there is, quite simply, no need for it; we 'know' what faith is and what beliefs we are required to subscribe to, and all that is necessary is obedient response. As a corollary of this, the whole purpose of the doctrinal structure of faith is seen as being to provide the boundaries. Doctrine and its acceptance functions as a defining mechanism for faith which is able to dictate who qualifies as 'in' and who therefore remains on the outside.

Secondly, in the service of this clear-cut doctrinal structure, there is usually to be found (although it may not always be clearly spelt out) a very simple and crude mechanics of the metaphysical 'how' questions which does scant justice to the complexity of the issues involved. So, for example, there are serious questions around concerning the corporeality of the resurrection, but these tend to be entirely dismissed from a literalist/fundamentalist standpoint: Jesus was raised physically from death, could appear and disappear, yet could eat fish and so on. To believe otherwise, in even the smallest detail, is to doubt the reality of the resurrection and smacks of heresy. Similarly the relationship of humanity and divinity in Jesus is, on the rare occasions when it is considered at all, inadequately kept in balance. This may be strenuously denied, but divinity almost always eclipses humanity, and to suggest that Jesus' humanity might have enabled him at any point to say 'No' to God is considered tantamount to blasphemy.

Thirdly, if the package of faith and its simple (indeed naïve) mechanics are to be 'true' then an utter reliance needs to be placed at all points upon the historicity of the Christian faith, and here, of course, doctrinal literalism most nearly shades into biblical fundamentalism. And so, for this form of faith, it matters that Jesus was born of a virgin, that he walked on water, that the stone was rolled away and the tomb empty and so on. These things become the touchstones of faith, and acceptance of the historical accuracy of the scriptural accounts feeds neatly back into the readiness to accept the whole doctrinal schema with which we began.

All of these three elements then operate together to create both a distinctive outlook within the individual believer and an equally distinctive atmosphere and ethos in the life and structures of the whole church. Because the basic framework of belief is so fixed and so unyielding, other aspects of church life are sucked into its ambit, such that certain ways of doing things or particular forms of worship become the 'right' ones, and key phrases or ideas may become, effectively, tests for membership

– and for membership read orthodoxy, or even, sometimes, 'true Christianity'.

At one remove from doctrinal literalism is ethical literalism. This too clearly finds its inspiration and origins in scripture, whose categorical statements – most especially those connected with sexual morality – form the unbending and unchanging framework for 'right living', just as the framework of doctrine provides the means of 'right belief'. Again there is no possibility of dissension or argument, since we 'know from the bible' that certain things are right and others wrong. To choose a current topical example, homosexuality is wrong 'because the bible says so'.

Thus far, however much one might dislike this approach oneself, one might well also have to concede that at least it has a certain naïve consistency about it. Just as in matters of doctrine, though, the mind-set which is inculcated by having such a narrow and clear-cut set of rules begins to take over in other areas also, and this has a tendency to produce two results, both equally unattractive and both, ironically, at least verging on being un-Christian.

The first of these is a propensity to extrapolate from the specific 'rules' of scriptural ethics precisely what God will or will not approve of in situations which are not treated of – and often never even conceived of – in the bible. This negates any sense of human partnership with God as we seek to discover his will in new and previously unknown situations, and it fails to do justice (as with doctrinal literalism) to the complex nature of modern ethics. It is, I believe, not possible simply to 'read off' God's will and a sense of right and wrong at the forefront of medical and technological ethics, or in specific situations which involve conflicting ethical demands. The only possible way forward is in an open, prayerful waiting upon God and, when we must choose to act in one way or another, to choose knowing that amid all the complexities we could, in good faith, have chosen misguidedly. Only time and the repeated exposure of informed and prayerful conscience to each new ethical challenge will enable us to discover how God's purposes may best be served and what love might mean in these new situations.

The second by-product of ethical literalism is the arrogant assurance of its own rightness which results in a harshly judgemental attitude towards those who do not share all of its convictions. Again the convictions provide a framework and barriers, outside of which exist all who do not agree with this standpoint and who are therefore, by definition, 'wrong'. They may be well-intentioned, they may be all sorts of things, but they are wrong just the same and they will eventually be judged as such and found wanting.

Finally and further removed again from the central reference point of scripture is what we have called here socio-cultural literalism. This is, in a sense, a mixture of doctrinal and ethical literalism, but it has lost its precise roots in these things just as it has to a great extent failed to retain its scriptural basis also. It consists, therefore, in a tightly defined and codified set of attitudes, structures and procedures which combine to produce a culturally specific way of life which is often only quasi-religious in origin – and certainly in affiliation – and owing as much to other cultural elements as to faith, and which, for precisely this reason, is often therefore something of a menace as far as faith is concerned.

It is always dangerous to cite an example in a case such as this, simply because it is inevitable that any group so chosen is bound to be annoyed by being portrayed in this rather unflattering light. Nonetheless, partly because an illustration is the clearest way of conveying what is meant by socio-cultural literalism and partly because I consider it actually to be true (and in its context highly significant), it appears to me from an Irish perspective that an almost perfect example of socio-cultural literalism is represented by the Orange Order and by the other associated Loyal Orders such as the Purple, the Black and the Apprentice Boys of Derry. Within these orders there is a self-contained world of quasi-religious and scriptural (though often neglected) origins, which is built up into a complete set of atti-

tudes and preferences (even prejudices) which are founded on
the rigid distinctions between 'in' and 'out', 'right' and 'wrong'
and which are, just as we have outlined earlier in connection
with doctrine and ethics, designed to operate negatively against
those who are out – in this case specifically Roman Catholics.
Orangeism may have had ('may' with a large question mark
being the operative word) *bona fide* religious origins, but these
have become so overlaid by political and social detritus that
whatever the Orange Order may itself say, it is hard to view the
order as authentically a Christian body; rather it is a socio-cult-
ural-political (and at best quasi-religious) organisation which is
increasingly a thorn in the flesh as far as all of the churches are
concerned, for where the churches wish to speak to one another
of the things of God, the Orange Order is prone to muddy the
waters by introducing a political or cultural dimension into the
discussion. It is more socio-cultural than religious, and religiously speaking it is, as we have claimed above, a menace.

The single factor which, more than any other, unites these
various forms of fundamentalism or literalism, is that their apparent aggressiveness and exclusiveness is in fact, as we
touched on earlier in this chapter, defensive. It is a reaction to
external pressure which leaves the believer or the group feeling
under threat, one response to which is to withdraw into the
security of what one thinks one knows and to condemn,
whether explicitly or implicitly, all those who do not subscribe
to this 'right' way of believing or of doing things.

This may well be a tempting response to pressure and may
also be a common one, but it is not in any sense a helpful or con-
structive one, since it merely produces, as we have observed, a
ghetto which is doomed sooner or later to shrink and perish.
Furthermore it is a ghetto which prohibits any further meaningful conversation with the world outside; all that is possible from
within its walls being a kind of war of attrition, and both the loss
of conversation and the draining effects of attrition have deleterious effects on the ghetto and the outside world alike. In the
long term no-one wins and everyone – in one way or another –

loses by this aggressively defensive (and often referred to as a 'siege-mentality') behaviour.

It is at this point that agnosis has such a vital contribution to make, and can offer a vision of faith in relationship with the world which is at once more courageous and, precisely because courageous, also more creative than any form of 'fighting retreat' can hope to provide. For it is certain that the various challenges and pressures which may be brought to bear on our faith must be met, and met as dynamically and life-enhancingly as possible. To retreat from them is, as we have seen, potentially disastrous; and neither will it do to ignore them and hope that they will simply go away, for they will not do so. The precise points at which pressure is exerted may vary from one generation to another, but that pressure will always be there, and on each occasion that Christianity does not react creatively to that pressure, credibility is lost which it may prove very difficult to regain retrospectively. Being wise after the event is nowhere near as effective as being even partly wise at the appropriate time.

A Christian faith which is grounded in an explicit acknowledgement of agnosis is in a favourable position to make such a dynamic and creative response. The key to this lies in the openness and lack of fear – and therefore of aggression – which agnosis engenders. Within the world of our faith, agnosis constantly acknowledges and indeed rejoices in the partial and provisional nature of everything, and recognises too that there is much which lies beyond the finite limits of our comprehension. All of the categories and concepts of faith, however venerable or revered they may be, are open to revision in the light of fresh inspiration. Faith is seen not as a closed system, but rather as an ever-changing organic reality from which we draw our religious life but which is in turn fed by our constant testing and questioning of it.

With such an attitude, this kind of unknowing Christianity is far less hostile and defensive than a more literalist form of faith, since there is nothing to be lost and everything to be gained from involvement with any and every realm of thought. We can afford to be courageous and both interrogate and allow ourselves to be interrogated by other disciplines and cultures, knowing that the perpetual search for a clearer vision of God and of truth is more important than the illusion of our own certainty; and we can, in this spirit, humbly learn from others what of truth they may have to teach us. And this, whilst it may reshape what we believe, will also undoubtedly enrich our faith.

Agnosis thus keeps alive – and indeed itself stimulates – conversation between faith and the world of ideas, and also between one faith and another or one church tradition and another. Furthermore it does so without prejudicing the outcome of these conversations, which would, of course, invalidate them from the outset. For agnosis enters such conversations knowing that whilst our faith may have much to offer to others, it is not, because partial and provisional, the 'last word'. It is open to the insights of others and may be changed by them, just as its own insights may inspire change in others.

The way of unknowing is content with this. It accepts that the Christian faith may emerge from these conversations (although, of course, in one sense it never emerges from them since they are ongoing) having changed or developed in some respects, or simply understanding something about itself in a different way. That this may be so is hardly to be wondered at, at least from the perspective of agnosis. For agnosis, as we have mentioned, views faith not as an inanimate object but as a living entity – or perhaps, more accurately, as something which has the potential for growth and development. That potential needs to be realised, and if it is not, then, as we stand still our faith will surely petrify with us and within us. But if we are seeking and developing spiritually throughout our life then it is natural (and desirable) that our faith should grow and evolve as we discern new things, test different aspects of that faith and experience God perhaps in fresh and surprising ways. As we do this we shall want to understand these things as best we may, and we shall undoubtedly continue to make attempts to give rational and coherent expression to our beliefs, and yet, if this same growth is always to continue we must have within us also the perpetual openness and creativity of unknowing rather than the aggressive, defensive and ultimately also fossilising influence of certainty.

# CHAPTER 7

# Two Conversations

In the course of examining some of the ills of fundamentalism and establishing by contrast what positive benefits agnosis can bring to faith in its relationship with the world, we have introduced the idea of the ongoing conversation which must take place between the world of faith and theology and a rich variety of other cultural and intellectual realms. Such interaction will be of benefit to both partners, not merely to theology, and it is therefore the intention in the present chapter to flesh out this notion of conversation somewhat and to explore in a little more detail what it might mean (and what part agnosis plays in facilitating it) in connection first with the world of science and secondly with the admittedly rather broad realm of the arts, and in particular literature and music.

Of these two areas, it is the arts which will concern us most extensively here. This is not to imply that theology has more in common with the arts than with the sciences, or that one relationship is more important than the other. Rather, it is for two very simple reasons. First, the relationship between theology and the sciences has recently been paid a substantial amount of attention by those who are far better qualified than I am to comment on the scientific end of things; and secondly, that the area of the arts and theology has received relatively little attention and, being an arts (specifically literature) graduate, this is the realm in which I am most at home and hopefully most competent.

As far as science is concerned, then, there is currently something of a relatively new rapport between theology and the sciences. That this should be so is possibly a little surprising given the squabbles between them in the past (in most of which, Christianity, or at least the church, has come off second-best), but it is nonetheless to be welcomed.

It is founded on a growth of mutual respect and a diminishment of fear as both disciplines have discovered that not only does the other have some merits in its distinctive approach and methodology, but also that the findings of each need not be mutually antagonistic but may rather be complementary and mutually enlightening.

From a theological point of view there has emerged, with the exception of the fundamentalist theological world as noted in the previous chapter, a new openness to the discoveries (and indeed the whole project and aims) of science. Theology has left behind its previous inherent tendency towards rejection and hostility in the face of new ideas and discoveries, and has grown largely to accept that such discoveries do not automatically threaten the credibility of the Christian faith even if, on occasion, they may profoundly affect our attitude towards one aspect or another of that faith. In essence two things have happened. Theology has learned (or perhaps is still learning) to accept and live with an ever-larger measure of agnosis in the many areas of faith which are not susceptible of proof, and it has learned also that scientific discoveries do not necessarily conflict with or undercut theology's own distinctive contribution to our understanding of ourselves and the world which we inhabit.

Both of these points are significant enough to deserve at least some amplification. Thus faith, and with it theology, have shown themselves at their best to be increasingly willing to recognise that this is what their subject matter is – faith, and not knowledge involving cognitive certainty or complete accuracy – and this acceptance of agnosis allows, in turn, for theology and science to run on parallel courses of discovery rather than on an ever more antagonistic collision course. Theologically it is gain rather than loss if science in any of its branches is able to answer questions about the nature of the universe or the course of history. We need not feel threatened, whether by the theory of evolution, or the 'big bang' theory, or by archaeological-cum-scientific discoveries about the extent of Noah's flood, the migration of semitic peoples in the ancient world or their religious beliefs and cultic practices. What is happening is that the 'how' and 'what' questions are being allowed to mingle with the 'why' questions. Previously what has tended to happen has been for there to be a power struggle between the two kinds of question: theology initially gaining the upper hand by laying claim to the answers to the 'why' questions, and then later, from perhaps the mid-nineteenth century onwards science fighting back and attempting to invalidate the 'why' questions by proving that religion has no satisfactory answers (indeed often patently inaccurate or mythical ones) to the 'how' or 'what' questions such as 'how' the world came to be and reached its present condition, physically and materially speaking.

Today, increasingly, whilst the distinction between the two types of question remains valid (and theology still deals more with 'why' and science with 'how'), both theology and science are more willing to admit the validity of the other's questions and even allow the other discipline to pose what each has traditionally seen as 'their own' kind of questions. Thus theology has stopped claiming historical accuracy for the biblical accounts of creation, for example, and regards the findings of science as illuminating. Scripture is then read as myth and the loving will of a creator-God allowed to be amazingly present throughout the still-continuing billions of years of creation rather than confined to a now discredited six day period. Science, in turn, is increasingly disposed to acknowledge the 'purposiveness' of creation and – without necessarily committing itself, although many individual scientists do – to consider seriously the possibility of a creative will which imparts that purpose to what might otherwise be a random cosmic accident.

Science too, then, has become more open, and this is ironically and almost poetically as a direct result of its own activities. The crucial discoveries in this regard have come in a branch of science in which I find myself – as would many theologians, I suspect, if the fact were admitted – woefully ignorant and uncomprehending. I cannot therefore comment meaningfully on the nature of the experiments involved, or even on the theories concerned, but only on the findings of those experiments as they impinge, at a level which I can understand, on theology and the world of knowledge in general.

The branch of science in which these insights have occurred is one which might initially be presumed to be light-years away, if the phrase is not too close to a pun, from theology: quantum physics and the world of sub-atomic particles. What has occurred here, as I understand it very much from a layman's point of view, is a discovery which has effectively revolutionised the whole understanding of science at every level, and radically changed its perspective on, and its assumptions about its own activities. This is the discovery that absolute objectivity (and therefore, logically speaking, absolute knowledge) is not available to us. It is simply not possible for us to obtain it. The effect of this is to undo the 'truth' upon which science had founded itself for well over one hundred years, and it is entirely to science's credit that it has assimilated this discovery more quickly and more completely than theology has ever succeeded in doing with the findings of science in previous generations.

The basis of this discovery is the realisation that at the level of sub-atomic particles, the mere presence of an observer has an effect on the behaviour of those particles, and therefore, by definition, we can never know exactly how those particles behave in the absence of an observer in and of themselves, but only how they appear to us to behave. Secondarily, but equally clearly, this principle is then transferable to our understanding of anything at all: whether because we materially affect things by observing them or whether because our findings are processed and interpreted by us, we never have absolute objective knowledge, but only human knowledge of things as they seem to us.

This is revolutionary enough by itself, but it opens the way for an exciting new development in our whole approach to 'knowledge' and therefore to the possibility of new relationships between different kinds of knowledge previously thought to be mutually exclusive because of the supposed distinction between objective knowledge and subjective conviction and commitment.

At the forefront of this attempt to bridge the gap is Michael Polanyi, a scientist-turned-philosopher, with his concept of 'personal knowledge' which is open also to ideas of faith and commitment even in science. Polanyi's work reflects both an exciting development in science and a new point of contact with faith, and it is valuable here to explore the connection a little more deeply since it helps to explain the new depth of interest which theology and science have for one another and also the relationship between objectivity and subjectivity in our estimate of knowledge, whether scientific or theological.

Thus our knowing involves, according to Polanyi, a number of things: apprenticeship to a tradition of knowledge, within which the scientist (in his case) dwells; the recognition of problems and the seeking for solutions, which demands the personal involvement of the scientist; the presence of tacit knowledge, which we are aware of but cannot adequately explain; and the presence of an hierarchy of levels of explanation which will not allow us to reduce different levels of knowledge to any lowest common denominator or reduce one level to another. How, it may be asked, does this 'personal knowledge' impinge upon Christianity? One of the best expositions of Polanyi's position and its relevance for faith is that provided by Leslie Newbigin:

> What, then of the objectivity of our knowledge? It is obvious, for example, that when conservative Christians insist that their Christian faith refers to objective realities, they are (rightly) seeking to deny the opinion that these Christian beliefs are simply expressions of subjective feelings or experiences and to affirm that they make contact with a reality beyond the self. But it is also clear that it is futile to deny the subjective elements in the Christian's confession. How does Polanyi escape from the charge that his epistemology of science would reduce science to a matter of subjective experiences? Polanyi's answer is twofold. First, he says that, al-

though all claims to know involve a personal commitment, the scientist makes them 'with universal intent'. For this reason he publishes them and invites all his colleagues to test and judge for themselves. Second, Polanyi says that the truth of the claim either will or will not be validated depending on whether or not it leads to further truth. A valid truth claim will lead to new discovery – often to discoveries undreamt of by the scientists themselves. The truth claims of scientists are thus not irreformable and indubitable claims to possess the truth; rather they are claims to be on the way to the fullness of truth. There is thus no absolute dichotomy, such as Descartes has bequeathed to us, between knowing and believing. Knowing always involves the personal commitments of the knowers, for which they are prepared to risk their careers as scientists.[1]

What is predicated here of the scientist and his personal commitment to knowledge might equally well be posited of the religious believer and his claims to religious knowledge. 'Personal knowledge' appears to be at least one place where the forces of personal conviction and commitment and the admission of ultimate agnosis and consequent provisionality can meet and complement one another creatively and profoundly both in science and in theology.

This new receptivity of science and theology to one another's insights and methods alike has had one further consequence which has, in a very real sense, cemented the rapport between them. This has been the shared development of a real appreciation of wonder (to which we have referred previously, especially in the writing of Michael Mayne) as an appropriate response to our experience of life. Both disciplines, in accepting in different ways the limitations of the knowledge available to them, have found themselves more able than previously to stand in awe of the miracle of all that is with its inscrutable mysteries and ravishing beauty and to marvel at the possibility (for science) or the conviction (for faith) of the loving and purposive will of God which undergirds it.

The mere fact of this drawing together of these two former adversaries is remarkable enough in itself, but what is of even greater significance are the benefits which have accrued to both partners from their union. For Christianity, it is evident from the large number of books which have been produced in recent years which have attempted to articulate a genuinely contemporary approach to a living faith, that Christianity has been stimulated to re-think many aspects of its own identity. Perhaps most of all it has been encouraged to shrug off any tendency towards passivity, and to begin again to perceive the Christian life as something dynamic and active as we constantly seek to discern God's will in the light of new situations and new discoveries – the area in which this is easiest to see being that of Christian ethics, which is continually being drawn into new evaluation and reflection by scientific advances in a multiplicity of fields.

Conversely, the world of science has been equally stimulated by being reminded of the existence of different levels of knowledge and of the importance of categories of thought such as 'faith' and 'involvement'. Likewise seeing the complementarity (rather than opposition) of the concepts of subjectivity and objectivity with regard to knowledge has kept alive the insight – which is reinforced by faith – that knowledge is not merely objective but is always potentially value-laden also.

Finally, both faith and science – or at least, many individual scientists – have responded with some enthusiasm to the revived notion of human partnership with God in creation, in ethics and in his loving purposes for all that is. From the perspective of faith and theology this partnership has been discussed elsewhere, its consequences being that faith is seen as alive, creative and, because creative, risky, rather than being envisaged as a monolithic 'package' which is simply 'passed on'. For science, the idea of human partnership with God allows science the humility of its own agnosis, and reminds its practitioners (and the rest of us) that there are responsibilities attached to the use which we make of its discoveries, the abnegation of which responsibilities was so accurately but savagely satirised by Tom Lehrer:

Once the rockets are up, who cares where they come down;
That's not my department, says Werner Von Braun.

Clearly, then, there are both sound reasons for, and solid benefits to be gained from the continuation of this rapport between
theology and the sciences. Equally plainly it is a rapport which is
most likely to be fostered if Christianity can learn to follow,
without fear and defensiveness, the way of unknowing. For,
quite simply, the more open and receptive our faith is, the richer
and more life-giving it will become.

If this conversation with the world of science is a relatively
new one, then in one sense at least the conversation between
theology and art is as old as belief itself. At the same time,
though, it is equally necessary that this conversation should be
given a new direction and a new impetus if it is to continue to
flourish in the future. The reason why this needs to be so is that
traditionally Christianity has tried to dictate the terms of its encounter with the arts just as much as it has done, until very
recently, with the sciences: an attempt at dominance which
springs from Christianity's supposed absoluteness, any claim to
which is, of course, rescinded once agnosis begins to be taken at
all seriously.

For most of the history of Christianity, therefore, the 'conversation' between theology and the arts has, in reality, been rather
more in the nature of a monologue. As Iris Murdoch puts it so
succinctly in *Metaphysics as a Guide to Morals*, ' … western art has
*served* religion and its dogmas'.[2] (Murdoch's italics.) Certainly
the relationship has been a fruitful one and has given rise to
some of the most wonderful and enduring art in every medium
which the world has ever seen, but the traffic has been unre-
servedly one-way. That is, Christianity has allowed itself to be
used as a rich quarry for artistic inspiration, and indeed it has
often encouraged such use by its patronage of the arts, but it has
not been in its turn receptive to any importation of artistic values or methods into its own world of faith.

This pattern of relationship deserves a little more examination here, in the course of which it will become evident why

change is needed, and how, as with the sciences, agnosis may help to facilitate such change. We have referred above to Christianity's perception of itself as absolute, by which is meant that traditionally the Christian faith has seen itself as having an ontological and epistemological primacy over every other discipline, faith, or realm of thought. In terms of the arts this has meant that Christianity is primary and art secondary. Art has all too often been viewed as being incapable of adding to or enriching faith, but merely of being inspired by it and reflecting something of the marvels which are already enshrined in that faith. Thus painters, sculptors, musicians and writers may draw from the well of the Christian faith, but their productions come from that faith rather than contributing materially to it. It is this perception which, I would argue, needs to change such that the conversation becomes a genuinely two-sided one, and if this is to happen (and it is possible to argue that it has in a small way already begun to happen) then much will depend upon the unknowing quality of our faith, for it is our acknowledgement of conceptual agnosis which will allow us the freedom to find our faith enriched in ways which are not ultimately reducible to words – or at least to rational argument and cognitive understanding.

Agnosis, whilst not denigrating the rational and cognitive aspects of faith, simply acknowledges that there are limits to our understanding and that not only will conceptual thought only ever take us so far, but also that even what is expressed in the form of concepts and ideas is inadequate and partial. Agnosis therefore welcomes the ability of the various arts to give expression to aspects of faith which are not dependent on cognition and which rest on other different but equally valid levels of apprehension of, and response to God.

Obviously in one sense the 'closest' of the arts to theology is literature, since it rests on the same verbal and grammatical framework, and this is therefore an excellent starting point for our examination of the conversation between art and theology as it reflects the diversity which is possible even within the constraints of the single medium of language, as well as indicating that theology is actually being most true to its task when it embraces the insights and methods of art as well as logical conceptual thought.

Literature then, whether prose or poetry, finds its religious reflection in the (until recently oft-neglected) literariness of scripture. For too many centuries scripture has been viewed as the repository of doctrine and 'truth' in a way which has largely obscured the beauty of the medium through which these things are expressed. Literature therefore at once offers us the chance to re-capture the distinctive artistic genius of scripture, and to articulate for today new stories, rhythms, metaphors and symbols which reflect upon or stimulate our response to God.

We have commented earlier in our discussion of the agnosis of scripture on the ability of story to go beyond rational explanation and to tease us with things which lie at the limits of our comprehension, as, for example, with the parables of Jesus. This power of story as a religious medium is being gradually re-discovered in the present generation, and a number of literary explorations of the bible which have appeared in recent years have added substantially to our understanding of the literary genres and genius of much of the bible.

Similarly, the world of literature is increasingly discovering that myth, symbol, metaphor and so on have the power to enrich faith through the offering of an aesthetic as well as a purely intellectual experience which allows us to respond to faith as a complete being rather than as a disembodied brain – which is all that is required for purely conceptual thought. This may perhaps be done in any number of ways, but there are two which suggest themselves particularly. One is simply through the versatility of story. We may, for example, be brought through story to sympathise powerfully with, or even to like, a character who then reveals him or herself as being capable of some immense evil or who has once committed one especially heinous act. In these circumstances our perceptions of good and evil and our whole scale of values is, if not brought into direct question, at least thrown into relief in a way which it is not possible to achieve simply by the posing of an intellectual ethical question. Similarly, we may follow in story someone's quest for good or their spiritual odyssey in search of God and may thereby be moved to embark upon or renew that search for ourselves, whereas any doctrinal recitation of the attributes of God is most unlikely to move us to anything like the same extent.

The second avenue by which literature has the potential to shape and inform our faith is simply through the beauty and magic of words themselves, pre-eminently (although not, of course, exclusively) in poetry, and their ability to capture a mood or a feeling and imbue it with powerful symbolic or allusive overtones and resonances. Here, perhaps, the power of language not merely to echo but actually to foster faith has been recognised for some time. There is a rich heritage stretching back to Herbert and Donne (and beyond) and which, during the past century or so has included such figures as Gerard Manley Hopkins and T. S. Eliot. In these and other great poets of the spirit the mysteries of faith are not merely voiced but explored and brought to new life and expression, and it is this process which must be continued today – as indeed it is by poets such as R. S. Thomas, and by novelists such as Flannery O'Connor, Walker Percy and, even despite herself, Iris Murdoch.[3] What is needed though is not so much a few isolated voices but a positive chorus as more and more people come to explore faith beyond the somewhat narrow and restrictive limits of purely logical and conceptual thought.

Finally, literature has, like all of the arts, a dynamic immediacy as it reflects (more directly and passionately, on the whole, than doctrinal statements) an individual's experience of God and of the spiritual life. In this it is, of course, like scripture itself; scripture being, as we have seen, more a record of encounter with God than a sustained theological treatise about him, and it reflects scripture also in the way that books by different authors will present different facets of that life and experience and interact creatively and illuminatingly with one another. To say this is not to elevate literature into some sort of quasi-scripture, but rather to indicate that it can enrich and enliven (and in ways which are usually non-cognitive, deepen our understanding of) our faith in a way parallel to that in which our faith is ever and again kindled and nurtured by the eternally fresh story and poetry of scripture itself.

What literature may do on a verbal level, art and sculpture are able to do on a visual level. At this point it is only honest to admit that whilst drawn to the world of literature and especially to the world of music, I am something of a philistine as far as the visual arts are concerned. It is thus harder to comment both on the 'effect' the visual arts may have on us and on the connections which this has with our religious sensibilities, but I can only hope that through listening to the experience of others some justice – however scant – may be done to this aspect of religious response which has proved so emotive and fruitful throughout the ages.

To the untrained eye at least, the distinctive genius of visual art lies in its immediacy – that is, its ability either to capture an otherwise fleeting moment or to encapsulate past, present and future in a single frame, and in both of these respects art is able richly to inform and inspire our spiritual life. Again, I propose to offer just two examples from the many – possibly more appropriate ones as far as connoisseurs are concerned – which might be cited. The first is the abiding genre of the Pieta. There, perhaps, in the hands of the greatest artists, the central defining moment in the story of our redemption has been caught and held. There, in the face of Mary, in the attitudes of those around, in the broken, bloodied lifeless form of her son is all the cost and the pain of the love which redeems all things. There too is the sorrow at the savagery of humanity and at the evil which has crucified Jesus in the guise of his brothers and sisters time and again since the world began. As we look we are brought at once to the heart of human evil and to the heart (and the cost) of love both human and divine, and we are moved and drawn in to share in the risk of the way of love in our own lives. And all of this is without thought, or conscious thought at least. We may go away and reflect on what we have seen and we may choose to verbalise to some degree the experience we have had, but the experience of the art itself stands without need of such verbalisation, and will almost certainly in its impact upon us inform and enrich our spirit at a level which is very different from that of cognition. Furthermore there will usually be a rich and fruitful interaction between our cognition and our more experiential or emotional faculties which will both refresh us spiritually and bring new life to our reflections on and understanding of our faith.

This process is so central to the notion of a conversation between art and Christianity that it is worth exploring it at least a little more closely. In what sense, then, is it that art (such as, in this instance, the Pieta) does not merely draw upon faith, but also in its turn enriches and indeed helps to shape it? The subject matter of the Pieta – the death of Jesus – together with all of the accompanying events including burial, and in due course, resurrection, is self-evidently crucial to the doctrinal structure of Christianity, both in terms of forming elements of the Apostles' and Nicene Creeds, and in the wider sense of being the raw materials which contribute to doctrines such as the incarnation and the doctrines of the atonement and redemption and resurrection. This doctrinal structure is important, but it is as we have argued on a number of occasions, only partial and provisional, and it is also, if taken purely in isolation, somewhat dry and dusty and hard to link meaningfully with the living world of human experience. But look again at the Pieta. There – without words or thought – is explored with richness and passion what this doctrinal framework means for us. The reality and pain of Jesus' death and the sorrow of the disciples is crystallised for us, and the power and wonder of the resurrection – which we know to be 'around the corner', as it were – is brought into glorious relief as we realise that it will break the power of this death and sorrow on which we now so painfully gaze. Theology is not neglected, but it is fleshed out, and the two-dimensional world of Greek and Latin metaphysics is transformed in the Pieta into the three dimensional world of human experience and feeling.

The Pieta, of course, is a distinctively religious – and specifically Christian – artistic form, and it is therefore not particularly surprising that it should have a dialogical relationship with our experience of faith and with its doctrinal structures. The second example which I have chosen to explore is perhaps, however, more surprising in that it is not overtly religious in anything like the same way, and yet is equally well able to inform our faith in certain essential respects. Rather than another genre, then, I have chosen a specific work of art, this time a sculpture: Michaelangelo's David, although, in a sense, one might just as well have chosen any great sculpture (or portrait) of the human form, whether male or female.

The major point at issue here is faith's (and with it theology's) relationship with the material world and specifically with the corporeality of human existence. At one level this should not be a problem, for a proper theology of creation will encompass the consistent emphasis of the first creation story in Genesis 1, 'God saw that it was good' – and indeed 'very good' in the case of the human race. However, as I have argued at some length elsewhere, Christianity has always tended to be a far more heavily 'salvation' rather than 'creation' oriented faith, and the balance between the two elements has often become rather lost. Salvation has taken over from – and in the process downgraded, and even denigrated – creation.

It is not difficult to see how this has happened. The concept of salvation carries with it the need to be saved from something, and this something has – all too often in the history of Christianity – been not merely 'evil' but rather the totality of our physical human condition which has been seen as essentially evil, or at least tainted by evil, in itself. We are creatures condemned for our lifetime to the evils of corporeality, and destined at death – if we have mortified our physical nature sufficiently during our lifetime – to be set free from the shackles of the body and given new life in the realm of the spirit, which, because incorporeal, is 'good'.

This may be a slight over-simplification of the process by

which salvation dominates creation, but it is nonetheless a substantially true picture, and what a far cry this overwhelmingly salvation based (and usually heavily Augustinian) understanding of faith is from God's mythical expression of the goodness of his creation in Genesis. Conversely, the visual arts – unless, of course, they are entirely abstract, although even then there is some connection simply through their use of colour, texture, shape and line – deal directly or indirectly with the material world both in terms of subject-matter and of medium, and are thus well placed to redress this imbalance and initiate a more two-sided conversation both between art and faith and between the 'creationist' and 'salvationist' strains within faith itself.

For what is Michaelangelo's David about? Yes, at one level it is a representation of a biblical character, but it is far more than that, and it is not to be limited in its significance by being chained to one particular biblical story or character; it is not merely a 'bible illustration', however sublime. David, surely, is a celebration of humanity in all its physical beauty and perfection, and equally a celebration of humanity in the almost incredible skills of brain, hand and eye which have been vouchsafed to us. This statue seems almost alive: the muscles ripple beneath the skin, the figure is poised to move with strength and grace, and there is instilled in us through the statue itself, and via it through its creator, a sense of awe and wonder at the almost unlimited richness (and goodness and beauty) of what it means to be a human being. And this in turn resonates with theological overtones: for neither David nor the genius which brought him to being speak to us of any evil inherent in corporeality or the material world; this is not something demonic to be redeemed from. Rather, there is a goodness and beauty about humanity which permits our human form and nature (and creative gifts) to be a medium through and in which God's nature is at once glimpsed and celebrated and reflected, and here, plainly, there are connections which one might almost explore for ever, with the doctrines of creation and incarnation.

David, then, and much other great visual art, has the potential (and certainly the power, through its effect on us) to assist in the healing of a disjunction at the doctrinal level of faith, namely this delicate balance between the so-called 'physical' and 'spiritual' worlds, and between the often conflicting doctrines of creation and redemption.

Whether in the form of the Pieta or David, visual art speaks to us in ways which are, in the first instance, beyond our cognition, and which can, therefore, take us beyond the limits of our understanding. For a faith which acknowledges its own limitations of knowledge and which allows a creative place for agnosis, the value of such a conversation is inestimable. Our hearts may be lifted to worship, to love and to service with a passion and a dynamism that a mere doctrinal structure (however necessary) is powerless to inspire.

Finally, I wish to turn to the realm of music, for it is here that I find some of my own most profound experience of God, and it is music which, perhaps more than any other medium, picks up (as Susanne Langer has observed[4]) precisely at the point at which words leave off. At this point, as I suspect in any discussion of the conversation between art and theology, there is a need to be somewhat personal, since whilst the doctrinal structure of faith is common to all believers, the ways in which this is informed and enriched from other sources such as the arts will vary tremendously from individual to individual. Thus my own starting point, in that it represents for me a perfect illustration of the capacity of music to speak to the spirit – and with a distinctively religious voice – is a scene from the film of Peter Schaffer's play, *Amadeus*. In this scene Mozart's wife, Constanze, has gone secretly to the court composer Salieri to seek his assistance, and has taken a sheaf of Mozart's manuscripts with her to let Salieri see his music. Salieri flicks through the pile of music (which plays on the soundtrack as he does so) and after a minute or so the manuscripts slip from Salieri's now literally nerveless fingers and, as he himself reels and stumbles under the impact of the music he has heard in his head, he says simply: 'I have heard the voice of God.'

With Salieri – and, I am sure with countless other music-lovers also – I would unhesitatingly echo these words whenever I am in the presence of great music, whether Mozart's specifically or that of many other composers also. And this reaction points us to something profound in the conversation between art and faith which allows Salieri's words to be not blasphemy, but rather, truth.

In this conversation there are two factors which need to be explored: the music itself, and the quality and nature of our response to it. As far as the music itself is concerned, the central question is: what is it about it which both evokes Salieri's (and our) response and which leads us to feel that such a response is justified? However, before this question can be satisfactorily answered we need at least briefly (and possibly contentiously) to consider what it is that music is capable of reflecting or communicating.

The answer to this, of course, is virtually anything – and certainly I would not claim that all music reflects or speaks of God. Music may embody almost any emotion or state which the human psyche or spirit is capable of experiencing. There is much twentieth century music, for example, which reflects the disjunctions and pain of life; there are specific works, such as Schumann's second symphony which seem to mirror scenes and states within the soul of the composer. Beyond this realm of the purely personal, music is also deeply embedded in and reflective of particular cultures and is able at times to bring them to rousing, and occasionally even rebellious expression. Works such as Finlandia and Ma Vlast (particularly Vltava) seem to speak directly from and to the soul of a nation, and for countless people the world over there is nothing so emotive as a National Anthem.

Music, then, it appears, speaks to us in an almost countless variety of ways, and plainly one would not wish to claim that this is always a reflection of, or portal onto divinity. To make such a claim would be sheer folly, for there is, and always has been in every generation, much music that is simply bad aesthetically and which speaks to us, if it speaks of anything at all, not of divinity, but of the superficiality or incompetence of the composer – and indeed, I would argue, ironically, that this applies to a good deal of contemporary so-called 'worship songs' and other popular church music.

At the same time I imagine that almost all of us know that Salieri's words ring true on at least some, perhaps even many, occasions when we are listening to music, and this begs the question posed a few paragraphs ago: what is it about music which evokes this response from us?

One might, in the case of Mozart, and doubtless a variety of other composers also, essay at least the beginnings of an answer by invoking such words as 'beauty' and even 'perfection' and suggesting that these qualities are reflections of God's beauty and perfection and that they therefore lead us, wordlessly and non-cognitively, back to him. My own feeling is that whilst there is undoubtedly some truth in this, it is at best a partial answer, for it does not explain why music which is not technically perfect and perhaps even music for which the word 'beautiful' is not quite apt can still nonetheless mediate something of God.

By way of an alternative, and hopefully more all-encompassing and satisfactory answer, then, it is worth reflecting for a moment not so much on music itself as on our varying response to it. At the most general level, then, there is a great deal of music which, although it could never be described as bad in the sense employed earlier, makes a relatively shallow impression on us: it may be pleasant enough to listen to but it does not move us or engage us significantly. It is, if you like, 'musical wallpaper'. Further than this there is music which stirs our emotions in some way and we feel the joy, the pain, the fervour or whatever is the underlying mood of the music. And beyond this there is music which does something quite inexplicable: it quite simply grabs our attention – our full and undivided attention – and takes us beyond listening and beyond feelings and into a space of stillness where there is only the music, and in which, in a curious fashion, we almost cease to be ourselves and the music be-

comes us and we become the music. It is here, I suggest, in this
total and ego-less attention to the music and the moment, that
without cognition (perhaps even without conscious recognition)
we meet with and hear the voice of God. How and why this
should be so is beautifully captured by Iris Murdoch in a passage from *Metaphysics as a Guide to Morals*:

> ... the (good) artist does not copy particular things, he sees
> and copies the Platonic Ideas (the universals or conceptual
> exemplars) themselves. The general notion of a spiritual lib-
> eration through art is accessible to common-sense as an ac-
> count of our relationship to works of art when the walls of
> the ego fall, the noisy ego is silenced, we are freed from pos-
> sessive selfish desires and anxieties and are one with what
> we contemplate, enjoying a unique unity with something
> which is itself unique.[3]

Admittedly Murdoch invokes the notion of Platonic Ideas, but
within a more overtly Christian context we might well substitute the idea of copying something of the sublimeness of God,
and equally, although she is discussing works of visual art, the
same principle undoubtedly holds good for our appreciation of
other forms of art also.

Experiences like this may foster and feed our faith and our
spiritual life both directly, in and of themselves, and by extension as they nurture our capacity to 'attend' in the more obviously spiritual aspects of our lives such as prayer. Within our
experience of music itself there is indeed a parallel with the attention of prayer in that we are drawn out of ourselves and tran-
scend the usual parameters of that self; and just how close that
attention is to prayer is illustrated once again by Iris Murdoch
when she says, rightly in my view, that, 'Prayer is properly not
petition, but simply an attention to God which is a form of
love.'[4] In music, then, we may be drawn by delight into attend-
ing to one reflection of God, and our quality of attention here
may in its turn foster a deeper attention when we come to attend
to God directly in prayer and in worship. It may be, incidentally,

that this is why some of the greatest music ever written is specifically religious music for use in worship (mass settings, motets etc), for here, of course, the attention to music and the attention to prayer are woven yet more intimately together, the music itself being a part of the church's prayer.

In yet another different way, therefore, music, like the other arts we have considered, offers us an experience of – or at least a potential awareness of – God, which is, by definition, beyond all words and therefore beyond all logical or conceptual thought. It is up to faith (and with it theology and the structures of the church) as to whether it is willing to accept this rich (and yet doctrinally unspecific and indifferent, and therefore potentially suspect) input or not. A rigidly doctrinaire faith will almost certainly feel the risks involved to be too great and wish to continue to try to keep science and the arts firmly (but increasingly unsuccessfully) in what it perceives as their place. Conversely, a faith which acknowledges its own agnosis will welcome it, for it will gratefully allow that since our knowledge (in cognitive terms) is partial and can only lead us so far anyway, then why should there not be other and complementary routes to experience of and knowledge (in the sense of personal rather than cognitive knowledge) of God?

Both this conversation with music and the other arts and the conversation with science need to be pursued ever more vigorously by the world of theology and faith, for both science and art in their different ways have much, it seems, to offer to a properly agnostic faith. What literalism and certainty may fear and wish to dominate, agnosis may humbly embrace and learn from.

# CHAPTER 8

# Living Agnosis

Thus far we have traced the history of agnosis in the bible and the succeeding Christian tradition and explored something of its potential for the life of the church and of the individual believer both in terms of its own identity and in terms of its relationship with other areas of life. What is necessary now is to indicate why such an agnosis is central to the task specifically of theology and to suggest what its effects might be if it were to be thoroughly integrated into that task. This, in essence, is the purpose of the present and succeeding two chapters.

I wrote at some length in my previous book, *A Space for Belief,* on the deleterious effects of bad theology and of a feeling that theology is currently in a time of some crisis. In the period since that book was written it has been interesting to see this view confirmed in a variety of places, and most recently in a volume of the Dominican journal, *Spirituality.* What is particularly interesting about this essay is that it reflects not one but a variety of voices, and that it locates the crisis precisely where I have argued that it exists: that is, in the inflexibility and narrowness of so much of our theologising. After a passing comment by Tom Jordan OP in his editorial, there is an extended discussion of the issue in a substantial article by Angela Hanley, which is, effectively, an extended review of a book entitled *Building Bridges: Dominicans Doing Theology Together.*

In the course of this essay she cites references by several contributors to the dangers of bad theology, and in particular she quotes Albert Nolan:

Much has been said and written about the crisis of authority and credibility in the church, the crisis in religious life, the crisis of faith in the West and the crisis created by Christian fundamentalism, but I would like to suggest that behind all of this there is a profound theological crisis.[1]

Of the reasons for this crisis Hanley herself then comments tellingly:

> We have bad theology because of the ruling structures of the church. The *Uno duce, una voce* type of leadership we have had, that took little account of the experience of specialist theologians to advise and guide, and which made a narrow orthodoxy the measure of loyalty, has brought us headlong into the current crisis of theology. Antonietta Potente echoes this: 'I feel there is a lot of fear and that some continue doing theology that lies somewhere between concrete dogma and superficial speculation, so as somehow to survive in the midst of post-modern fashion and ancient traditions. There are those who continue to confuse thirst with relativism and, because of this, they continue launching anathemas and forbidding new thoughts of the poetry of theological work.'[2]

Admittedly this is written from a Roman Catholic standpoint, but something very similar might be said from within any other of the major churches.

In such a climate a theology based upon agnosis is perhaps at once unlikely to be popular and yet more essential than ever before. I have discussed elsewhere the crisis of relevance to which theology has been brought by its inflexibility and often academically rarefied nature,[3] and we have now reached the point where we can begin to see just how radically this theology would change (and needs to change) if given a substantial admixture of agnosis.

At the present time our doctrinal formulations (and with them our whole way of approaching our faith and prayer and worship) are couched in the timeless forms of ontology and classical metaphysics: that is, the relationships within the Trinity are of a certain sort, the incarnation 'worked' according to a certain model, and so on. These formulations are venerable and have been helpful to many, but they are all too often viewed as exclusive and sacrosanct: this just is what God is like, and our relationship him just is of a certain (and usually totally subservient) kind.

The function of agnosis is not to undo or to denigrate these formulations, but rather to enable us to understand them more constructively and to sit somewhat looser to them than has frequently been the case. This is necessary both from the perspective of theological honesty and integrity and also for the enrichment of our theology by enabling it to become more receptive to the diverse theological and spiritual voices of different cultures, life situations and individuals.

As far as the first of these requirements is concerned, agnosis is of value as a consequence of its affinity with negative theology which is itself too often neglected in the quest for (necessarily spurious) certainty. Of such a negative theology Oliver Davies remarks incisively:

> Negative theology critiques the many positive ways in which we are able to speak with, to and about God that are given through scripture and theological tradition, reminding us of the provisional character of all theological language and preserving the essential mystery of God-with-us.[4]

This is not to devalue the attempt to speak positively of God, but merely to remind us of the provisional nature of these attempts.

The second requirement, that of listening to other voices, in a sense flows from this, for if our formulations and statements are provisional then there is no reason why they should not be refined or re-interpreted by every new theological voice. It is, as Marcus Braybrooke puts it, that:

> We are ... beginning to recognise that truth is multi-faceted and that the true and living God transcends all human description and language. Instead of thinking in rigid terms that one view is right and another wrong or one belief is orthodox and another heretical, we are learning that different theologies, be they feminist, classical, black or liberation, can add to the fullness of our understanding of God's revelation in Christ.[5]

Taken together, this provisionality and plethora of voices should alert us to the true nature of all of our theologising and even of our most hallowed doctrinal statements. Helpful they may often be, but they are not final and somehow ontologically correct. In reality what they are is not a set of ultimate and absolute definitions, but a series of images and models which provide pointers and glimpses to aid our understanding and, as Stanley Hauerwas pertinently reminds us, our prayers.[6]

This being so, our theology (and even our classical doctrinal formulations) are no longer set in concrete. I am not suggesting that they should be abandoned, for there is much wisdom in them, but we are not in thrall to them and they are not the only possible expressions of our faith. In principle – and hopefully also in practice – there is no reason why other pictures and models should not be created which might provide complementary insights to those generated by the classical models.

Indeed it is encouraging to see that over the last thirty years or so this has been happening with increasing frequency, both within particular theological cultures such as liberation theology and feminist theology, and within what might be called the 'classical western tradition', if this term is not too offensive to these other varieties of theology. Thus, for example, Jürgen Moltmann has re-discovered the reality of a passible God,[7] and more recently J. Denny Weaver has provided yet another possible interpretation of the mechanics of atonement.[8] In the same vein I am currently working with a new series of ideas in the realm of Christology and exploring whether the fixed ontological categories of Christ-ship are necessarily the most useful or whether there is theological mileage in the idea of Jesus of Nazareth 'becoming' the Christ rather than simply 'being' the Christ.

This freedom, which owes much to agnosis, is to be welcomed, and with it the increasing number of pictures and models which may help to feed our faith. The simple fact of there being many possible models should serve as a reminder that none of them is definitive and correct, and that all are flexible and provisional.

The fact of this freedom and provisionality in turn generates a renewed interest in the whole question of what theology – and more specifically doctrinal studies – is for. What is the purpose of our doctrinal statements? Traditionally, and working from within the (supposed) realm of a fixed ontology and metaphysics, the function of theological/doctrinal statements has been seen as that of providing the right content for belief: that is, as imparting whatever conceptual knowledge of God and of our relationship with him it is necessary for us to have in order to exist within the household of faith. Indeed, very often its function has been interpreted even more rigidly than this, as providing the only set of beliefs which must be held in order to be saved. Thus the opening of the Athanasian Creed proclaims, 'Whosoever will be saved, before all things it is necessary that he hold the catholic faith; which faith except every one do keep whole and undefiled, without doubt he shall perish everlastingly', after which it proceeds to detail exhaustively the precise qualities of God in which we are to believe.

Contrary to this traditional understanding, however, I would argue that this sort of apparent certainty is not available to us, and that our formulations, models and pictures cannot offer us a definitive 'blueprint' of God which is to form the precise content of our belief. Instead, I suggest, our doctrinal statements exist primarily to offer us pointers to and patterns of relationship with God. Thus, for example, as I have argued in *A Space for Belief*, our perception of God as the Trinity of Father, Son and Holy Spirit informs and guides our prayer as it creates a relational framework within which we approach God. Knowing the limitations of our cognitive knowledge, agnosis re-shapes our faith to become more a matter of personal knowledge and relationship – which is what it was always supposed to be anyway, although this was often hidden by the insistence on the minutiae of right belief. What happens is that, as Marcus Braybrooke neatly expresses it, we recognise that, 'Christian faith is not, in the first instance, acceptance of certain intellectual dogmas, but trust in the Living God,'[9] and that, 'Revelation is not truth about God, but encounter with the Living God.'[10]

Such an understanding, which has, I think, been foreign to us for some generations and is still foreign to many today, is, as we shall see in the next chapter, much more creative than a rigidly conceptual faith of certainties, and it is also substantially more faithful both to the self-understanding of the early church (followers of 'The Way', not a system of doctrine), and to the characteristic teaching and calling of Jesus himself. Certainly Jesus taught his disciples, but he signally failed to teach them much metaphysics, and he initially called them not by requiring them to subscribe to a detailed and precise set of beliefs, but simply by the command, 'Follow me'. Faith, looked at in this light, is less concerned with beliefs *about* God and Jesus, and more concerned (in the sense of experiential trust rather than conceptual knowledge) with belief *in* God and Jesus.

If we can allow our perception of faith to be re-drawn in this way then it will become (or at least is likely to become) at once less anxious and thereby more positive in its outworking in the lives of believers and church alike. That this should be so is, I think, obvious. For if faith is seen as a fully worked-out scheme of 'factual' conceptual beliefs then there is, for each of us, a degree of anxiety as to whether we have believed exactly the right things or are able fully enough to believe some of the things which we are required to believe; but conversely, if faith is seen as primarily relational rather than cognitive then we are set free from this anxiety and our doctrines are simply more or less useful in communicating personal and relational knowledge which informs and enriches our own unique relationship with God.

Perhaps again at this point a disclaimer is necessary. I am not setting aside or attempting to invalidate our doctrinal statements or credal formulations, and these things remain entirely valid. All that I am advocating is a review and consequent redefinition of their status and purpose. All of Christian doctrine remains a legitimate subject for discussion, though not any longer for narrow dogmatism, and the more useful pictures and models this discussion generates the better.

In this more agnosis-dependent and more overtly relational

concept of faith we can (and must) acknowledge that there is much about God and indeed about the *telos* of human life that we do not know with any degree of certainty, and that the pictures which theology has traditionally employed are just this – pictures, and not any sort of definitive or absolute map.

Perhaps the best way to illustrate this is to look briefly at three doctrinal areas which are connected directly with our salvation, these being, in turn, what it is that we are saved from, the 'mechanics' of the incarnation, and the nature of the resurrection.

Traditional Christian theology has had very firm ideas on all of these topics. With regard to what it is that we are saved from there has been little doubt that this has been a very real and graphically depicted hell. The precise details may have varied a little over the ages and according to personal taste, but there is a recognisable common content which links the patristic period, medieval wall-paintings, Dante's *Commedia* and the hellfire sermon in James Joyce's *Portrait of the Artist as a Young Man*. Hell has been seen as an objectively real entity with a wide spectrum of specific torments, demons and so on.

Admittedly in this case agnosis is only one of the factors which mediates against the retention of such a scenario – both common sense and an appreciation of the essentially loving nature of God do so also – but agnosis has a vital place in that it encourages us not so much to dispense with this doctrine but to acknowledge its significance even whilst radically re-interpreting it. Thus the doctrine of hell has, I think, rightly divined that millions of Christians have felt, and still continue to feel that they have indeed been saved from something. This much is genuine Christian experience. What agnosis refuses to do is to flesh this out too literally and insist on the exact nature of what this something is. It may be that we are delivered from simple extinction, or from the eternal absence of God, or if we are to think in more contemporary post-Freudian psychological terms, even from ourselves – and most of us know that the worst of ourselves is not a little dark and frightening. Literal demons may be present no longer, but in mytho-poeic form they may still serve to remind us of the fear, pain and darkness from which we know ourselves to be delivered by our life in Christ.

For all but the most thoroughgoing of fundamentalist Christians, some sort of reinterpretation such as this is probably common currency, and people are using – even without knowing that they do so – the tools of agnosis. However, things become, I suspect, a good deal more contentious when we move on to the second of the areas I have highlighted for discussion: the incarnation, and specifically the Virgin Birth of Jesus, for this is plainly a central piece of doctrine, directly referred to in the historic creeds of the church.

At the same time, however, it is also a doctrine which has proved, and continues to prove, a stumbling block to a substantial minority of otherwise committed believers, and it may be that the concept of agnosis can offer us a creative solution to the difficulty.

At the outset it should be remembered that even the scriptures themselves do not speak with one voice on the subject of the Virgin Birth, and in enshrining this doctrine in the creeds what has happened is that the voice of a few has been taken and made *de facto* the voice of all – whether or not they find themselves able to assent to it. Within scripture almost the whole of our 'evidence' for the Virgin Birth comes from just two of the gospels, those of St Matthew and St Luke. The other two gospels and St Paul in his letters not only take no interest in it but also show no sign of knowing anything at all about it. Indeed, a strong case could be made from the opening of St Paul's Epistle to the Romans ('descended from David according to the flesh') that St Paul simply assumed that the conception and birth of Jesus took place in the usual fashion.

Faced with this diverse array of approaches in scripture we may surmise that, just as St John does with his prologue and as St Mark does with his bold and arresting opening sentence ('The beginning of the gospel of Jesus Christ the Son of God'), St Matthew and St Luke were not so much recording simple 'facts' as employing images and ideas to reflect and highlight the unique nature of Jesus. Yes, the Virgin Birth may be true, but it does not have to be so, and it may equally well be a brilliant stylistic device to arrest the reader and point him or her to something which is far more important – the significance of the message and actions of Jesus. Agnosis does not discount the possibility of a factual Virgin Birth. Rather, it simply says that we cannot know, and that there is room for a variety of interpretations gathered around the common theme of what the story (factual or mythical) is attempting to convey to us. The message of the Virgin Birth (who Jesus is and why this is significant) may remain central and non-negotiable, but the 'mechanics' of this birth and the status of the story as fact or myth may be allowed to be open, may be, in the useful but too often neglected term of the reformers, allowed to remain among the *adiaphora* of church teaching.

If the Virgin Birth is potentially contentious, then the doctrine of the resurrection is a theological minefield. Not only is it witnessed to throughout the entirety of the New Testament and central to the creeds, but it is in a very real sense both one of the most distinctive beliefs of Christianity and one of the most crucial. Without it Christianity would, effectively, cease to exist, except as a series of ethical precepts and exemplars. As so often, St Paul expresses it most appositely: 'If Christ has not been raised, your faith is futile and you are still in your sins. Then those also who have fallen asleep in Christ have perished. If for this life only we have hoped in Christ, we are of all men most to be pitied' (1 Corinthians 15:17-19).

Since this doctrine is so vital to the whole fabric of Christianity it may well be asked why there is any need to approach it in a spirit of agnosis – indeed, is not any tampering with it merely presumptuous? Not so, I would argue, for what we may well wish to be agnostic about is not the reality of the resurrection (about the centrality of which I entirely agree with St Paul) but the precise nature and form which the resurrection took with Jesus and will take with us.

To begin with Jesus himself. The gospel narratives depict a whole complex of phenomena in describing the resurrection: an empty tomb, the stone being rolled away, angels (or young men) clad in white, appearances behind closed doors, the cooking and eating of fish and much more. For some people, admittedly, none of these 'events' poses any problems; but for other people some or all of these details are impossible to assent to as objective 'facts', and yet they still wish to continue to proclaim Christ's resurrection. Such a position will immediately be dubbed as heretical by the more conservative elements in the church; yet again agnosis enables us with integrity to affirm the reality of Christ's resurrection even if we may feel the need to remain unconvinced by specific details.

Earlier in this study, in chapter two, we discussed the initial faltering nature of the new resurrection faith: mistaken identity, complete failure to recognise Jesus, inability to believe initial reports and so on. Thus even within scripture itself there are hints that agnosis and a less than full understanding of the exact nature of resurrection are perfectly valid responses to that event. Further than this, though, as with the Virgin Birth, agnosis is not discounting the possibility of a bodily resurrection exactly as depicted in scripture: it is simply saying that we cannot know, and therefore we cannot make belief in every last jot and tittle of the scriptural accounts into some kind of test of faith.

Again it is important to attempt to understand what it was that the New Testament writers, and in particular the four gospel writers, were attempting to communicate, and we need to appreciate that our modern sense of genres such as history and biography is far removed from theirs. We naturally tend to assume that the gospel writers were endeavouring to produce a factual historical account of events 'as they happened'; that they were, in essence, first century biographers or journalists. To assume this is to read our perceptions back into another earlier, and foreign, world. It is very much a similar case with the resurrection as it was with the Virgin Birth. In each instance the gospel writers, through their depiction of it, were trying to give

voice to something far more important than the supposed cir-
cumstantial details of it. Thus with the resurrection what they
were witnessing to was their absolute conviction that their crucified friend and master really was alive again – and what better
way to do this than in stories which reflect (and depict) the
experience of meeting with him. This sense of meeting and
being with the risen Christ is what is central to faith, not whether
he actually appeared in such and such a form and said and did
particular things. The stories may be recollections of events, or
they may be pictorial expressions of a deep inner conviction:
which of these, some or all of the individual stories are, we cannot be sure, and, for agnosis it does not matter very much anyway. Whether Jesus did and said particular things (especially in
the unique circumstances of his post-resurrection existence) is
mere speculation, and is of little or no consequence. What matters is the reality of his resurrection life as it made itself felt to the
first disciples and to us and, as David Jenkins said at the end of
one of his highly controversial Easter sermons (an ending which
is usually forgotten): 'If you have encountered the risen Christ in
the course of your life, then the rest is all speculation and none of
it really matters at all.'

If a substantial degree of agnosis is necessary with regard to
the resurrection of Jesus then it is even more necessary in any attempt to explore what the concept of resurrection might mean
for ourselves. Here too there is an orthodox received opinion reflected in the creeds – 'I believe in the resurrection of the body' –
which is very frequently (and again usually by the more conservative and evangelical sections of the church) interpreted in a
very literal sense, a sense which is then insisted upon as being
necessary for orthodoxy. More realistically, however, the truth
is that even if we wish to predicate some form of corporeality to
our own resurrection life, we can have no possible conception of
what this might mean. There is no point in adducing the resurrection body of Jesus, for even if we wish to interpret this entirely
literally it remains true that it was assumed for the express purpose of being again on earth and therefore gives us no clue as to

what form a 'heavenly' body, or in Pauline language a 'spiritual' body might take. It seems reasonable to assume that as our faith is a relational one, then heaven will be a 'place' of knowing, of recognition and of relationship; but what form these things will take is, in our present life, entirely unknown to us.

To put all of this into a more personal framework, certainly I believe in resurrection, and believe further that this involves some sort of sentient and inexpressibly rich life, but precisely what form (and, if embodied, then how precisely so embodied) this life will take, I can as yet have no idea. In this aspect of faith my agnosis, just as much as my commitment to the belief in resurrection, is, and must be, complete.

In all of these areas, and many more, then, being ready to approach our faith with a measure of agnosis frees us from a rigid dogmatism, allows us not to insist upon the exclusive and absolute 'rightness' of any one interpretation, and enables us to approach doctrine not as a system of rigid propositions to be believed exactly but as a series of models and pictures to facilitate our approach to and encounter with God.

To such a faith it matters very little that we cannot know certain (indeed many) things. What we are saved from or what precise form the resurrection took (and, for us, will take) is of no real concern. What actually matters – and in our personal knowledge of this we can rest content with not knowing much else – is the experiential and relational truth that we are redeemed into life. This, for believers the world over, is simple Christian experience, and it has always, I would argue, been the experience of Christianity at its best.

Quite apart from the fact that it is less rigidly doctrinaire and therefore exclusivist than a more conservative understanding of faith (though the two things are, of course, connected), a conception of faith such as this is also entirely more positive than a less agnostic and more 'certain' one. Thus in the case of salvation, Christianity has, for far too many centuries, been bedevilled – it seems a peculiarly apposite word! – by the thought of what it is that we are supposedly saved from, and faith has all

too often ruled (and been ruled) by fear; a fear which then infects
all other doctrinal areas also, since these must be believed in
exactly the right way if this fate is to be avoided. Agnosis opens
this prison of fear and liberates us to focus more on the positive
experience of what we are redeemed into: that is, knowing and
experiencing ourselves as being loved and graced members of
God's people, empowered as well as commanded to live in such
a way that the love and grace which we receive is shared fully
with others and thereby in turn nurtured once more within ourselves even as it is shared with others. It is, in St John's reported
words of Jesus, a vision of faith which resonates with the intention of Jesus himself: 'I came that they may have life, and have it
abundantly' (St John 10:10), and, 'These things I have spoken to
you, that my joy may be in you, and that your joy may be full'
(John 15:11).

There is a good deal more to be said on the nature and effects
of a more agnostic faith, and this will form the substance of the
succeeding chapter. By way of conclusion here, however, it is
sufficient to highlight one other effect of agnosis (apart from the
positive emphasis just outlined) upon our faith. And this is simply to make it less of a closed and exclusively 'confessional' circle and therefore more open and receptive to yet further ideas
and interpretations. If we can accept a degree of agnosis about
the 'how' type of questions (how did the incarnation work; how
does resurrection come about and take form) and attend more to
our positive experience of redemption and love in Christ, then
we will almost certainly find that our faith is less fearful and defensive and comes to have room for the views and experiences
of belief of others.

In the first instance this would be of benefit within
Christianity itself, for it might enable different theological and
ecclesiological groups to stop demonising one another; and it
might indeed have a substantial effect upon our whole ecclesiological self-understanding. (This topic forms the main subject of
the third of this series of books, *The Seeking Church: A Space for
All*.) Even beyond this, though, there would be ramifications as

far as inter-faith dialogue is concerned, for agnosis, whilst it would still wish to attest to the uniqueness of Christ's nature and work, would not wish to claim exclusivity for this as far as God's revelation of himself to humankind is concerned. The voices and insights of other faiths might then be welcomed rather than merely tolerated or even shunned. These faiths, just like Christianity, proclaim and mediate an experience of God, and this experience might be drawn upon and rejoiced in, rather than first making differences of belief – at least some of which may well be in the province of agnosis anyway – the first and only touchstone for the evaluation of experience. This is something which Timothy Kinahan explores with some thoroughness and wisdom in his book, *A Deep but Dazzling Darkness: A Christian Theology in an Inter-faith Perspective* (Dublin, The Columba Press, 2005).

Thus we are led inexorably to the question which underlies the content of the next chapter: if faith is not, principally and in the first instance, a schema of 'right belief', then what precisely is it, and how is it best understood in the light of agnosis?

# CHAPTER 9

## *The Freeing of Faith*

At the end of the previous chapter we posed the question: 'What is faith?' It might appear that this is a question which should have been framed at the outset of this study, but there is in fact a coherent internal logic which has delayed the consideration of this problem until now. In brief, this logic is that it is precisely agnosis which assists us in reaching our understanding of the nature of faith, and therefore it has been important to pay a substantial amount of attention first to agnosis itself and only then to turn to what faith is seen to be in the light of it. To have started with a definition of faith would have involved setting up what might well have been a misleading definition, since the argument of this book is that faith cannot be appropriately understood without admitting – and in substantial measure being defined by – the underlying concept of agnosis. Agnosis is not a bolt-on addition to a previous structure: it is itself fundamental to that structure.

In the minds of many believers, however, and one might add, in the collective mind of the hierarchies and governing bodies of most ecclesial communities, agnosis and an understanding of faith very rarely seem to keep close company, and faith is most usually defined in the conspicuous absence of agnosis. A useful starting place, then, now that we have taken full cognisance of the nature and broad effects of agnosis, is to look at the general nature of such understandings of faith and to see how they may be – or rather will need to be – refined by contact with agnosis.

In what might be termed, without, I hope, being offensive, the 'popular mind' and also within the official documents and self-understanding of many, if not all, of the churches, faith is associated primarily with a system of belief. This applies both across the broad spectrum of the churches, and within individual church communities or communions. Thus across the churches there is the common core of Christian belief as expressed in the historic creeds (Apostles' and Nicene); beliefs which are adhered to in all of the Christian churches, even if in some of the free or more evangelical churches the creeds themselves are not recited as such as a result of a dislike of fixed forms of liturgical worship. In such cases the beliefs are still in place even if the specific form of words is not.

Similarly within the individual churches there is frequently some form of confessional statement, such as 'The Thirty Nine Articles of Religion' within Anglicanism or the 'Westminster Confession' in the Presbyterian Church. These documents further define the specific beliefs and practices of a particular church, and usually do so in overt contradistinction to the beliefs of other churches and most especially the Church of Rome. These statements, while they do not have quite the status or weight of the creeds, nonetheless help to set out the precise identity and self-understanding of each church.

In both of these instances (creeds and confessional statements) the impression given – which may or may not reflect the intent of those who first framed the documents – is that matters of right belief are seen as entities of the first order. Right belief, it appears, and the 'correct' expression of that belief take precedence over all other concerns. Whatever it is that these beliefs are intended to lead on to or foster – whether this is commitment, trust, good works or whatever – is left to fend for itself in a very clear second place. What actually matters for membership of any church, and therefore, presumably, for salvation, is the correct theological and metaphysical 'knowledge' and the belief that this 'knowledge' is both true and accurate.

The effect of this is to make knowledge and acceptance of these beliefs into some sort of a test for membership. Recent liturgical revisions have removed the most blatant examples of this from the services of initiation, but it remains true that one is required to assent to a collection of very specific articles of belief in order to claim membership of the church. Within my own Anglican Communion this sense of knowledge and right belief being the test of membership is most overtly set out in Holy Baptism One and Confirmation One, both of which services are still in print and indeed still in use within the Church of Ireland. The process begins in the 'Charge' read to the parents and god-parents by the priest, the second part of which reads: 'Ye are to take care that this Child be brought to the bishop to be con-firmed by him, so soon as he can say the Creed, the Lord's Prayer, and the Ten Commandments, and be further instructed in the Church Catechism set forth for that purpose.' This same theme is then recapitulated by the bishop in the service of Confirmation: ' … the Church hath thought good to order, That none hereafter should be confirmed, but such as can say the Creed, the Lord's Prayer, and the Ten Commandments; and have been further instructed in the Church Catechism, set forth for that purpose.' There is, admittedly, a certain amount in the Catechism which touches on matters of relationship with God, but it remains true that the vast bulk of the requirements for membership of the church is concerned with propositional knowledge and assent to the proclaimed truths of the church.

As we have seen throughout the course of this study, however, it is simply not possible to present the concept of faith as a series of absolute beliefs in this way. From the perspective of agnosis, a system of conceptual beliefs cannot be of the first order, for we cannot make such absolutes out of entities and realities about the exact nature of which we, in the last resort, know so little. Contrary to the apparent packaging of faith in doctrinal state-ments and creeds, cognition in matters of faith is, and must be, of a second order status.

If this is the case, then we must return to our original ques-tion, 'What is faith?' and seek for an alternative answer which is consonant with the degree of agnosis which we must bring to that faith. The result is at once a new freedom for faith, and the rediscovery of an old but oft-neglected understanding of that faith. For what we are led to discover is that essentially faith is not principally concerned with belief (in the sense of assent to propositional knowledge about), but rather with belief *in*, and that therefore it is intimately connected with the ideas about the relationality of faith which were developed in the previous chapter. And this would appear to have been the nature both of the initial flowering of Christianity and of the Jewish faith from which it sprang.

In the case of Christianity this is immediately obvious both from the gospels and from the portrait of the emerging church in The Acts of the Apostles. As far as the gospels are concerned, we have referred already to the almost naïvely simple relational calling of the first disciples by Jesus: there is no teaching, no prior knowledge, no cognitive requirement, just the command, 'Follow me!' A comparable simplicity exists in Acts also, in that almost all of the preaching recorded there takes the form of – or at least includes – a straightforward re-telling of the story of Jesus, and it is to this story and not to any prior metaphysical speculation or rigorous conceptual schema that the hearers are invited to respond. Interestingly, it is on, I think, the one occasion that preaching becomes more abstract than this that it fails, on the whole, to convince. This occasion is St Paul's celebrated sermon at the Areopagus, recorded in Acts chapter seventeen, which attempts to relate Christianity to the current philosophies (especially Stoic) of the day. At the end of this sermon (which actually does not mention Jesus by name) we are told that: ' … when they heard of the resurrection of the dead, some mocked … but some men joined him and believed' – a stark contrast to various other occasions when we are told such things as, 'so those who received his word were baptised, and there were added that day about three thousand souls' (2:41) and, 'many of those who heard the word believed; and the number of the men came to about five thousand' (4:4).

That this emphasis on story and relationship should be present in Christianity is hardly surprising, for it sprang from a

faith in which these things were highly prized. Certainly
Judaism had its beliefs about God, but the essence of the Jewish
faith was (and is) not beliefs but a belief in God which is expressed through recounting the story of what God has done for
his people. Thus the Hebrew scriptures themselves continually
hark back to foundational events, and the Psalms, for example,
are full of references to the deliverance of Israel from Egypt.
Indeed, even credal statements are told through the medium of
story, as, for example, with the passage familiar to many people
through its frequent place in the liturgy of Harvest Thanks-
giving:

> A wandering Aramean was my father; and he went down
> into Egypt and sojourned there, few in number; and there he
> became a nation, great, mighty, and populous. And the
> Egyptians treated us harshly, and afflicted us, and laid upon
> us hard bondage. Then we cried to the Lord the God of our
> fathers, and the Lord heard our voice, and saw our affliction,
> our toil, and our oppression; and the Lord brought us out of
> Egypt with a mighty hand and an outstretched arm, with
> great terror, with signs and wonders; and he brought us into
> this place and gave us this land, a land flowing with milk and
> honey. (Deuteronomy 26:5b-9)

This emphasis on story in both Judaism and Christianity be-
tokens a very different primary understanding of faith from that
which can all too easily be promoted by an emphasis on creeds
and doctrinal formulations. Certainly these creeds and formulations are still present, but both their function and their status
have changed. Faith is seen to have more to do with experiential
categories such as trust, commitment and love than it has to do –
in the first instance, at least – with precise conceptual knowledge.
Understood in this more experiential and relational way, the beliefs themselves assume a second order status and their function
is no longer to define, but rather to assist us in forming clearer
(although still partial and incomplete and provisional) pictures
and models which will nurture and encourage our faith.

This clearly applies in areas such as the doctrine of the atonement, where theology has habitually spoken of models and acknowledged that there are several different possible and all equally acceptable understandings of the 'how' of atonement. However, it also applies to other doctrinal areas where we have previously been used to thinking more in terms of definitions. Thus, to take a central example, we confess belief in God as Trinity not primarily to form a series of definitions in the style of the Athanasian Creed, but rather to give expression to two enduring insights about how God appears to us to be and how we experience ourselves as relating to God.

First, then, it has seemed to Christians right from biblical times – as indeed it had seemed also to their Jewish forbears – that God is not a simple monolith, but has various modes of activity or faces, that is, *personae* in the classical terminology. In brief these faces are first, the creator and sustainer of all that is; secondly, the incarnate redeemer of humankind; and thirdly, the dynamic and life-giving Spirit by whom Christians have always felt themselves to be indwelt and empowered. To these faces or *personae* we have applied respectively the appellations of Father, Son and Holy Spirit, terms which have ever since assisted Christians in making coherent sense of their ongoing experience of God.

If the first function of the doctrine of the Trinity is to encapsulate something of how God appears to relate to us, then the second function is to proclaim that this relational quality of God is not something contingent (that is, something which might have been different and just happens to be this way) but is part of the essence of God's being. Thus the model of the Trinity asserts that within his own being God is already and necessarily relational – an assertion which is even more beautifully made in St Augustine's likening of the Trinity to, 'The Lover, The Beloved, and the Love which flows between them', an analogy which I have previously commented on at greater length in *The Right True End of Love*.[1]

In both of these respects the model of God as Trinity is instrumental in both shaping and nurturing our faith, but it does not and can not depend upon the precise accuracy of all of the Graeco-Latin metaphysical and philosophical terms through the medium of which it has, historically, been expressed. However technical and apparently hair-splitting these terms may be, they nonetheless do not add up to anything approaching a binding or absolute definition of God. All that they do is to impart at least some degree of clarity to a model which helps at once both to express and further inspire our belief in God as a God who creates, loves, redeems and indwells.

Viewed in this light, faith, even in its most apparently precise doctrinal formulations, ceases to have the spectre of a test lurking somewhere within it or just behind it. Instead it is set free to become something more creative and adventurous. This is a freedom which artists have known and embraced for centuries in their depictions of the things of faith. As Peter S. Hawkins notes:

> ... the painters of the German Middle Ages portrayed Christ's nativity in snow, with wise men who look like hearty northern princes and the Virgin a blonde Hausfrau. This is not, I think, a case of simple anachronism; it is, rather, a bold appropriation of the ancient story for the here and now in which the believer lives.[2]

But now this freedom applies not only to the ways in which we may represent our faith in the arts, but also to the ways in which we may live that faith in our churches and our daily lives.

Our faith becomes not an external parcel of beliefs to which we must subscribe, but rather a creative partnership with God, and, to use an idea much beloved by the early Celtic Church, an ongoing pilgrimage or *peregrinatio*. This journey of faith will involve us in doing two things of which Christianity has frequently been somewhat chary, but which nevertheless have almost endless potential for the enrichment of that faith.

The first of these is to rejoice in and to use our freedom to find new ways of expressing our faith which will communicate that faith effectively to others in an endless variety of life-situations. That this is necessary is neatly if somewhat starkly summed up by Marcus Braybrooke: 'Today new ways are needed to communicate the significance of Jesus,'[3] a statement which applies not just to the person of Jesus but equally well to almost any aspect of faith.

There may be several reasons for this need. The most obvious of these is that, without exception, our major doctrinal formulations are couched in language and ideas that are, quite simply, no longer common currency or even, one suspects, meaningfully understood by the overwhelming majority of believers. Both the doctrine of the Trinity and the doctrine of the incarnation are problematical in this respect. It is not my purpose here actually to create new models for understanding, but simply to point out the need for them, and it would plainly be of benefit if, alongside the classical metaphysical models, some new ones could be brought to expression which might reflect more contemporary modes of conceptual thought and expression.

Another possible reason for needing to reinterpret and re-express our doctrinal framework is that the traditional modes of doing so may turn out to be less than helpful for certain people. I have touched on this in *The Right True End of Love*, but another and more specific illustration comes to mind here. Thus not only are there specific individuals for whom the concept of God as Father, for example, might be antipathetic, but there are also whole cultures – or at least sub-cultures – for whom this is the case and for whom, therefore, new modes of expression and understanding will need to be found. It was, I think, the evangelist Nicky Cruz[4] who, on returning to the kind of gangland city areas in which he grew up, realised that the notion of God as Father was repellent to almost everyone he was talking to. Fathers were drunken, loutish, brutal, unreliable and often absent – hardly the ideal model for the God about whom Cruz wished to preach. In response to this problem he therefore developed the very local model of 'God the Gang-leader', a figure who was immediately comprehensible and who stood for qualities such as security and care, and was a figure to whom one vowed obedience. Of the models which we may create, some may be as local as this one, while others may come to have a wider appeal and significance. What is certain is that we need to continue creating fresh models and modes of expression in order continually to refresh and nurture our faith and even gain fresh glimpses in our understanding of it.

The second of the activities to which we are called by this new vision of faith is concerned not with the articulation of that faith but with its relationship to the world around it, and specifically with its ability to learn, where appropriate, from that world. St Augustine wrote of wisdom that:

> In Greek the word 'philosophy' means 'love of wisdom', and it was with this love that the *Hortensius* [by Cicero] influenced me ... The only thing that pleased me in Cicero's book was his advice not simply to admire one or another of the schools of philosophy, but to love wisdom itself, whatever it might be, and to search for it, pursue it, hold it, and embrace it firmly.[5]

All too often Christianity has mistrusted – or even shunned – the discoveries of science, the celebration of human creativity in the arts, and the reflections on life of philosophy. Augustine in his *Confessions* here reminds us that, as we saw in chapter seven, the Christian faith has much to gain from being in open dialogue with all of these things, and equally much to lose if it is unwilling to take the risks which that dialogue necessarily involves.

That there are risks involved can hardly be denied, but again for agnosis this is not a problem: indeed, it is simply a consequence of the fact that the whole of our faith is a risk – in the end we could be wrong! Further than this, though, our risk of faith is a reflection of God's own nature as risk-taking and thereby empowering rather than restrictive and domineering. This nature is expressed both generally in creation and specifically in the incarnation.

The risk involved in creation is both enormous and obvious,

for we believe first that God created us in love with the specific purpose that we should respond to that love with love. As the Westminster Catechism (in both its longer and shorter versions) puts it right at the outset: 'Q. What is the chief end of man? A. Man's chief end is to glorify God, and to enjoy him for ever.' Secondly, we believe that we are created as beings endowed with free will. There is therefore no guarantee (and daily experience both of ourselves and others amply bears this out) that the purpose of God's creation will be adequately fulfilled in any given life or community. God has taken the risk of conferring upon us at once the responsibility of implementing his will, and the ability to frustrate that will, and further taken the risk that there is no coercion involved as we freely choose which path to follow.

A similar situation exists even with regard to the unique circumstances of the incarnation. We are so accustomed to this that we often read and think about it as though things 'had' to be this way, and we thereby fail to appreciate the degree of risk and freedom involved. For things did not have to be this way: they were not pre-programmed and there was no 'fail-safe' mechanism. Right at the beginning, Mary could have said, 'No' to the angel; and similarly if Jesus was, as we profess, genuinely fully human, then even if he never said it and never even wished for a moment to say it, there must have been at least the possibility that he could at any point have said 'No' himself. Even here at the heart of the drama of human redemption God took the ultimate risk of making the realisation of his will and purpose completely dependent upon freely given human co-operation and loving obedience.

God's risk of faith in us enables us to be creative and adventurous in our faith in him. The nature of that faith relationship is perhaps most vividly depicted in the familiar parable of the talents, St Matthew's version of which reads:

> For it will be as when a man going on a journey called his servants and entrusted to them his property; to one he gave five talents, to another two, to another one, to each according to

his ability. Then he went away. He who had received the five talents went at once and traded with them; and he made five talents more. So also, he who had the two talents made two talents more. But he who had received the one talent went and dug in the ground and hid his master's money. Now after a long time the master of those servants came and settled accounts with them. And he who had received the five talents came forward, bringing five talents more, saying, 'Master, you delivered to me five talents; here I have made five talents more.' His master said to him, 'Well done, good and faithful servant; you have been faithful over a little, I will set you over much; enter into the joy of your master.' And he also who had the two talents came forward, saying. 'Master, you delivered to me two talents; here I have made two talents more.' His master said to him, 'Well done, good and faithful servant; you have been faithful over a little, I will set you over much; enter into the joy of your master.' He also who had received the one talent came forward, saying, 'Master, I knew you to be a hard man, reaping where you did not sow, and gathering where you did not winnow; so I was afraid, and I went and hid your talent in the ground. Here you have what is yours.' But his master answered him, 'You wicked and slothful servant! You knew that I reap where I have not sowed, and gather where I have not winnowed? Then you ought to have invested my money with the bankers, and at my coming I should have received what was my own with interest. So take the talent from him, and give it to him who has the ten talents. For to every one who has will more be given, and he will have abundance; but from him who has not, even what he has will be taken away. And cast the worthless servant into the outer darkness; there men will weep and gnash their teeth.' (Matthew 25:14-30)

Obviously one cannot push parallels too far, and one would not wish directly to allegorise this parable and say, for example, that the master is exactly an image of God, yet it nonetheless sheds some light on our relationship with God. Viewed in this way, our faith is not a fixed and immutable entity which we inherit ready-made and which just is, and must be guarded closely as such. Instead it is something much more organic than this, something which grows and develops over time, and something in which we are encouraged not to be afraid but to create and to take risks as we seek to discover the presence and will of God in every new unfolding situation.

Indeed, if there is any place at all in faith for fear, it is not – as so often Christianity has seemed to think – in creativeness, new-ness and even experimentation in theology and spirituality, but in allowing these things to become fixed and even fossilised. A living faith will grow and develop both in its efforts to model and picture its theology, and in its efforts to find how best to trust in and express God's loving will in countless new ways. An immutable faith may be a great deal easier to handle, but we will ultimately find that the God at its heart will be an idol of our own devising and not the unsearchable mystery of the living God. Agnosis may cause discomfort at times, but even that in it-self is a sign of life; and if our faith cannot move then it may well have passed, to misquote St Paul, 'from life to death' and become a fossilised schema of beliefs rather than a life-giving belief *in*. It is to a fuller consideration of the contours and implications of such a belief in that we must now turn.

# CHAPTER 10

# *A New Understanding*

In the previous chapter we have paid some attention to the primary character of our faith (and the nature of God) as being relational, and explored how this leads us away from focusing narrowly on belief and much more towards the powerful idea of belief *in*. It remains, however, to delineate just how thorough-going and all-encompassing this change is, and to reach an understanding of how it comes to inform and undergird our whole experience of faith and of God. In the course of this chapter we shall discover the full extent to which we are defined, given identity and held in being by our relationship with God and by God's own prior and intrinsically relational nature. In the course of what follows, I am following the general outline and using a substantial amount of the material included in an address to a diocesan clergy conference in May 1999 by the Bishop of Tuam, the Rt Revd Dr Richard Henderson. The almost complete absence of direct quotation is explained simply by the fact that I am working from notes made at the time and from memory, and not from a written text of the address.

I have already argued that agnosis resists the false certainties of precise conceptual knowledge and prefers instead the creation of models and pictures, and in the previous chapter at least some of the qualities inherent in the doctrine of God as Trinity were looked at. In the course of that discussion I argued that relationality is of God's essence, but the truth of the matter goes even further than this in insisting on the primacy of this relationality over any more cognitive process. For, given the experience and consequent modelling of God as Trinity, we see that God's own identity is given and defined by relationship: relationship is prior to all else. It is not just one among many characteristics of God; it is a (possibly even the) primary and defining one. For the Father is only the Father in so far as he is the Father of the Son; the Son is only the Son in relationship to the Father; and the Holy Spirit is not some sort of free-floating entity, but the Holy Spirit of God.

If God is thus characterised by relationality, then it is hardly surprising that we are defined by it also. We acquire our identity in community rather than in isolation, and it is other people's perception of us which accounts, from our very earliest and un-remembered days, for a large part of our self-image and self-understanding. Similarly we understand ourselves as we move among many other people and discover and appreciate the myriad similarities and differences between ourselves and them. So much does our identity depend upon community that it has proved to be the case that prolonged periods of solitary confine-ment are capable of seriously damaging identity, and, less graphically, it is likely to be true that any identity acquired in isolation from others – if such a thing is even really possible – will be a false and therefore potentially destructive identity. So our identity as much as God's is founded on relationality, and as we shall see, our identity is itself dependent on the relational nature of God.

It was, I think, Thomas Torrance who elucidated the nature of grammar as being the hidden patterning and governing schema which makes sense of language. That this is so is ex-tremely easy to demonstrate. Without grammar even a simple utterance becomes entirely obscure. Thus the words, 'London go will to you' are capable of being structured in either of two utterly different senses: as a command, 'You will go to London,' or as a question, 'Will you go to London?' Without grammar to order our words and provide us with tenses and so on, language as a series of disconnected words is more or less entirely mean-ingless and is certainly incapable of being the medium of any sustained connected thought or communication.

In a very similar sense, God's being and activity may be seen as the 'grammar of relationship' (definitely a phrase used by Bishop Henderson). It is God's identity as relational which sets the grammar of life and which offers us a framework for meaning – and just as with the doctrine of the Trinity in this and the previous chapter, this model of God as the grammar of relationship opens up the possibility of new models in answer to the question of what we are saved from and redeemed into which have been discussed earlier in this study. For faced with this framework of meaning, imparted by our relationship with the prior relationality of God, we are constrained in every ongoing moment of our lives, to choose between two alternatives. We can choose to live within that framework of relationship and the meaning which it imparts to human lives, or we can step outside it into isolation. What implications this has for our identity has already been touched upon, and we may simply note here that this 'outside' will be a place of non-communication (because of the absence of relationship) and of consequent disorder and anarchy; and, indeed, also of meaninglessness as in the example of the 'non-order' of words referred to above.

There is a tangential but essential link here with the primacy of agnosis in faith. The connection is that, amongst many other things, agnosis moves the ego, the 'I', away from the centre of things to the margins such that faith involves (as spirituality has always known) a degree of 'unselfing'. The reason for this is precisely the lack of absolute certainty which agnosis involves. The more 'certain' and propositional faith becomes, the more likely it is also to become something which I cling to, and of which I become fiercely possessive. Why this should be so I have explored in some detail elsewhere,[1] and it is sufficient to note that such a faith will be almost aggressively defended as 'mine' whenever any potentially corrosive or critical influence is perceived to be threatening it. It is almost as if the ego, the 'I', is responsible for defining the faith and thereafter of preserving it in a fixed form. Conversely, in a faith which is shot through with agnosis and which is more relationally orientated, it is, as we are coming to see, rather that faith is a part of what defines me and my identity is dependent upon and secondary to the identity of God and my relationship with that identity. An agnostic faith is not one which is jealously and fearfully guarded as 'mine', but one which can change and adapt in the presence of relationship and conversation with others of all faiths and none since, as Augustine reminded us earlier, it rejoices in 'wisdom' wherever it is to be found.

That an agnostic faith is primarily relational is of immense significance, for the 'opposite' of relationship is pride – the 'I' or the ego placing itself not alongside and in relationship with others, but over against them. This is painfully and patently obvious in the extreme instances where obsessive megalomania or paranoia comes to rule a personality such that the individual's own fame, power, or safety or whatever supplants all other considerations and feelings and becomes the only source of motive and action in that person's life. Yet equally, though less dramatically, it is also true in smaller measure in all of our lives. There are moments or periods when our own selfishness or self-importance causes us to disregard the needs or preferences of others and leads us to act as if we were the only person who mattered, and as if, indeed, the other did not really exist – as, for us, at that moment, they do not.

This pride is utterly destructive of relationship. The 'other' is consistently devalued and at times even hated. Indeed the only way in which the other can be tolerated is if they are capable of being subsumed into our own wishes, and any difference between me and the other will not be acceptable, for by definition this difference is a difference from the 'me' who constitutes the governing norm. If this pride is allowed to roam unchecked, the end, for each of us, is an entirely isolated and solipsistic universe which, through the lack of any relationship, totters on the brink of and will finally fall into the abyss of meaninglessness.

For all the bleakness of this picture, however, there is a final revelation imparted by a thoroughgoing relational (and necessarily, as we have argued, agnostic) faith. And this is that God's own prior relationality is able to heal our pride and destruction of relationship and thereby restore meaning – and here again we are led to new models, in this case of the atonement. On this account of faith, then, something very specific happened on the cross and in resurrection. There, in the person of the incarnate Son, Jesus, God took (and of course continues to take) all of our fragmented pride and hatred into himself and unites himself to us with a total all-embracing relationship there (Jesus' death and resurrection were not for some, but for all) and invites each of us again to enter afresh into relationship with him and with each other through grace.

This process can be seen in microcosm in the persons of the two crucified thieves:

> One of the criminals who were hanged railed at him, saying, 'Are you not the Christ? Save yourself and us!' But the other rebuked him, saying, 'Do you not fear God, since you are under the same sentence of condemnation? And we indeed justly; for we are receiving the due reward for our deeds; but this man has done nothing wrong.' And he said, 'Jesus, remember me when you come into your kingdom.' And he said to him, 'Truly, I say to you, today you will be with me in paradise.' (St Luke 23:39-43)

One of them is so locked into his own suffering and with it his own complex world of pride and hatred that he joins with the many in the crowd who are taunting and railing at Jesus. The other, however, is (even if possibly only momentarily) sufficiently freed from this ego-ridden perspective to perceive both the innocence and the identity of Jesus: he has fully entered into the presence of the 'other' and his request is a directly relational one, and he receives therefore the promise of redemption in and through this new relationship – 'You will be with me in paradise'. Here is the final triumph of God as the 'grammar of relationship': there is no life and no situation which cannot be transformed and imbued with hope and life and given meaning precisely through a new relationship with the perfect relationality of God himself.

At this point the various threads of agnosis and relationship (and the perceived nature of God) begin more obviously to interweave. This interweaving begins with the total relationship – both in the sense of being for all people and in the sense of encompassing and overcoming all situations and all of our frailties and evil – inaugurated by the death and resurrection of Jesus. This new quality of relationship achieves, in particular, two things as far as our conception of and experience of faith are concerned.

First, as we have touched upon already but need to elucidate more fully here, we are at once called and empowered to have the freedom and courage to experiment, create and even make mistakes in our theology, spirituality, liturgy and ethics. The ramifications of this are widespread, and the implications enormous for almost every aspect of our church life. To begin with we are, amongst other things, encouraged to take risks and to be increasingly open (remembering yet again St Augustine's words on wisdom) in our encounter with other faiths. This is something which is extremely difficult for an understanding of Christianity which experiences and expresses faith primarily as a series of propositions. After all, if I put forward any proposition then it must, by definition, be either right or wrong, and if another faith questions the validity of this proposition, then again that faith's position is either right or wrong. Just how rigid Christianity can be in this regard was demonstrated to me very recently by a letter which I received criticising some of my more liberal views and declaiming that 'Ecumenism [never mind inter-faith dialogue!] should have no place within the church'.

In contradistinction to such an inflexible attitude as this, agnosis and relationality allow between them a much greater degree of flexibility. Because there is much that we do not know there is almost infinitely more room for *adiaphora*, and because relationship is prized, in the end, above propositional statements, the experience of God in other faiths comes to be valued more highly than conceptual and doctrinal differences. Thus, for example, there may be many points of divergence particularly from the non-theistic forms of Buddhism, but there may still be much to be learnt from its wisdom and techniques on matters of attention and contemplation.

Similarly, and more parochially, the various Christian denominations might, if more attention were paid to both agnosis and relationship as the fundamentals of faith, place less stress on their confessional differences and requirements for unity, and more emphasis on their recognition of each other's undoubted experience of God. Both the inter-church and the inter-faith dialogues are subjects in their own right, and much more will be explored in the final volume of this trilogy, but here it is sufficient merely to note this possibility and potential.

Alongside this freedom to unlock the barriers which separate us from other confessions and faiths, we are likewise empowered to create new models and pictures through which to express and communicate our faith. This, of course, is nothing intrinsically new. It has been done in very specific circumstances by courageous individuals such as Nicky Cruz, and it has also been done by whole groups of theologians addressing the particular needs of certain cultures or sections of society such as Liberation Theology, Feminist Theology and Womanist Theology. What is needed now is an appropriation of this freedom and courage by not merely some but every form and school of theology. And, importantly, success or universal acceptability cannot and should not be the governing criteria for this experimentation.

That this is so has already been demonstrated by the various cultural-specific theologies referred to above. Thus, for example, Liberation Theology, especially in its earlier days, was seen by other forms of theology to be, on occasions, too extreme in its pronouncements, whilst yet opening up a rich vein of theological exploration. The result has been that many of the insights of Liberation Theology have survived and been incorporated into other forms of theology, while other elements (such as its early predilection for revolution and its condoning of violence) have not stood the test of time. And this sort of pattern is exactly as it should be.

It is also exactly what we should expect if theology generally finds the courage to develop new ideas and modes of expression. Plainly it is not possible to predict in advance what these will be, or how they will fare when exposed to the criticism of other theologies, but many of the ideas expressed in the present series of books are a kind of 'test case' for this. Some of these ideas are, I think, new, as are some of the means of expressing them; others are contemporary formulations of pre-existing (though sometimes newly rediscovered) ideas. Of these various ideas, some will turn out to be valid and useful, others possibly not so. But in a flexible and agnostic faith this is quite acceptable. None of these ideas claims to be a correct or absolute proposition; instead, each of them simply attempts to offer a means of approaching, understanding or communicating something of the mysterious reality which we call God.

The final outworking of this freedom and creativity in theology is a practical one which 'cashes out' in the sphere of ethics. I have argued at length elsewhere[2] that ethics must be rooted in theology rather than in, for example, a naïve and circular appeal to scripture, and if that theology is one of agnosis such as we have outlined here, then the ethics which is founded upon it will also be flexible and creative.

Such flexibility and creativity will apply both to what might be called existing ethical discussions, and to new ones as they arise in such realms as medicine, technology and the biological sciences. As far as existing areas of ethical debate are concerned, I have no intention here of repeating the substantial arguments expressed in *The Right True End of Love*, and it is sufficient to indicate that a faith founded in agnosis and relationality has considerable potential for revisiting and rethinking a wide variety of ethical situations, not least with regard to the many vexed issues of sexual ethics.

Perhaps even more importantly, though, our faith continually (and increasingly) needs these qualities of flexibility and creativity to response sensitively to an ever-growing plethora of entirely new ethical situations and questions. There is no easy answer to many of the questions which arise at the cutting edge of such things as biology and medicine, and in each case there is a wide variety of different – and possibly conflicting – dimensions to be considered. What is the potential benefit of any new technique or technology? Are there negative implications for any life or lives? Does the likely gain appear to us to outweigh any negatives? And so on. What agnosis and our new freedom in faith allow us to do here is at once not to pre-judge on simplistic *a priori* grounds, and also to allow for the possibility of mistakes and consequent re-estimations of what constitutes ethical behaviour in any given situation.

At this point, where we have charted the presence of agnosis in both the conceptual (belief) and the practical (ethics) aspects of faith, we are led to the second of the changes (and benefits) which a primarily relational approach to faith confers upon us. In essence this is simply the fact that not only is such a faith necessarily an agnostic one, but it is also one which experiences this conceptual agnosis as a positive rather than a negative thing. And it is positive because it is precisely this quality of agnosis which has freed us from bondage to propositional 'knowledge' about God and led us towards a refreshing and life-giving new emphasis on relationship with God at the heart of our faith. It is agnosis which has brought us to focus on this rich living experience of relationship which is, and must be, prior to any attempts to formulate that experience in cognitive and doctrinal terms. The concept of orthodoxy may be neat and tidy, but agnosis and experience remind us that the reality of relationship with God is at once both infinitely richer and a good deal more untidy.

So it appears that agnosis has brought us to a variety of re-evaluations and re-examinations. Faith is seen to involve not so much belief as belief *in*; it is not a fixed entity which is monolithically 'mine', and rather than it being defined by me it turns out that I gain my identity within it; and our faith is understood as being primarily characterised by relationality, love and commitment, rather than by the acceptance of an abstract set of supposedly metaphysically and ontologically 'true' statements. In the

course of this study we have, if not re-defined, at least re-interpreted the concept of faith, and it now remains to ask what the
contours of the theological and ecclesiological landscapes look
like in the light of this re-interpretation.

# Conclusion

Much of the task outlined at the conclusion of the foregoing chapter is the concern of the third book in this trilogy, *The Seeking Church: A Space for All.* What remains to be done here, however, is to see how far we have come thus far, and to indicate, at least briefly, the way ahead.

Thus in the first book in this series, *A Space for Belief,* the intention was to explore in fairly broad terms what the overall function of theology is and how it is related to different areas of the Christian life. In summary, this function was seen to be not to tie us down with a set of rigid and immutable dogmas, but to create the 'space for belief' of the book's title.

Following on from this, the present work has indicated the nature of the theology which is required if this 'space for belief' is to be a reality, and it has also delineated some of the characteristic features of a faith which is informed by such a method of doing theology. In this faith the concept of agnosis has been found to occupy a central place, and therefore it has been important to indicate that this is not a radical, new and dangerous idea, but one which has always been present within Christianity, although it has all too often been merely a hidden or submerged undercurrent within that faith. This is essentially the point reached by this book, and both faith and theology have been treated largely from an individual perspective – that is, we have explored their implications more for the individual believer than for the church at large.

But, of course, the fact is that the nature of the faith held by individuals will inevitably affect the nature of the church, since it is those individuals who are, corporately, that church.

Furthermore it will affect not only the nature of the church but its own self-understanding and its way of living and expressing its corporate theology. There will be implications for how the church sees itself as functioning, and what models it employs to understand itself. There will be internal ramifications in terms of how it thinks of ministry, both lay and ordained, and there will be consequences in the realms of both inter-church and inter-faith dialogue.

All of these things will form the substance of the final book in this trilogy. For the present, we may end here in the rediscovery of a valuable but often neglected dimension of faith, which, while it may at times be disconcertingly provisional, is at once truer to the ultimate mystery and transcendence of God than is an immutable faith of 'certainties', and also rejoices in the immanence of that same God in the all-embracing relationship of love. For both agnosis and relationality are likewise content that love should thus take precedence over propositional knowledge.

# Notes

INTRODUCTION

1. John Polkinghorne, *Reason and Reality*, (London: SPCK, 1991), p 15.
2. Hooker, *Lawes of Ecclesiastical Polity*, 1.2.2.
3. George Pattison, *The End of Theology -- and the Task of Thinking about God*, (London: SCM Press, 1998), p xi.
4. Søren Kierkegaard, 'Fear and Trembling' in *Fear and Trembling and The Sickness Unto Death*, trs Walter Lowrie, (Princeton NJ: Princeton University Press, 1941 & 1954), p 130.
5. Pattison, pp x-xi.


CHAPTER 1

1. Stephen R. White, *A Space for Belief*, (Dublin, The Columba Press, 2006) pp 80-81.


CHAPTER 2

1. Michael Mayne, *This Sunrise of Wonder*, (London: Fount Paperbacks, 1995), p 10.


CHAPTER 3

1. Maurice Wiles, 'Belief, Openness and Religious Commitment', *Theology*, Vol CI, No 801, May/June 1998, pp 163-171, p 171.
2. Augustine of Hippo, *Confessions*, trs with Introduction by E. B. Pusey, 1838. Reprinted in the 'Everyman' series. (London: J. M. Dent & Sons Ltd, 1907,) Book I:IV, p 3.
3. Oliver Davies and Fiona Bowie, *Celtic Christian Spirituality*, (London: SPCK, 1995), pp 1-2.
4. *Irish Church Hymnal*, 1960, Hymn 327, v. 8. Anonymous old Irish.
5. *Irish Church Hymnal*, 1960, Hymn 323, v. 7. Attributed to St Columba.
6. Herbert McCabe, 'Thomism', in *A New Dictionary of Christian Theology*, Ed. Alan Richardson & John Bowden, (London: SCM Press, 1983), pp 568-571, p 569.
7. John Macquarrie, *Two Worlds Are Ours: An Introduction to Christian Mysticism*, (London: SCM Press, 2004).
8. *The Cloud of Unknowing*, trs Clifton Wolters, (Harmondsworth: Penguin Books Ltd, 1978 & 1980), pp 67-8.
9. Rowan Williams, *The Wound of Knowledge*, (London: Darton, Longman and Todd Ltd, 1979), p 169.
10. Ruth Burrows, *Guidelines for Mystical Prayer*, pp 101-2, Quoted in Rowan Williams, p 168.
11. Michael Ramsey, Ed. Dale Coleman, *The Anglican Spirit*, (London: SPCK, 1991), p 20.

CHAPTER 4

1. Martin Henry, *On Not Understanding God*, (Dublin: Columba Press, 1997), p 111.
2. Tom F. Driver, *Christ in a Changing World*, (London: SCM Press Ltd, 1981), p 7.
3. Michael Ramsey, Ed. Dale Coleman, *The Anglican Spirit*, (London: SPCK, 1991), pp 91-2.
4. Stephen R. White, *The Right True End of Love*, (Dublin, Columba Press, 2005), chapter 5, pp 58-68.


CHAPTER 5

1. Timothy Kinahan, *A Deep but Dazzling Darkness: A Christian Theology in an Inter-faith Perspective*, Dublin, The Columba Press, 2005, p 12.
2. Cf such works as: Michael Mayne, *This Sunrise of Wonder*, and Gerard W. Hughes, *God of Surprises*, (London: DLT, 1985).
3. G. K. Chesterton, *Autobiography*, (London: Burns Oates, 1937), pp 94-5. Quoted in Michael Mayne, *This Sunrise of Wonder*, (London: Fount/Harper Collins, 1995), p 7.
4. Michael Mayne, p 17.


CHAPTER 7

1. Leslie Newbigin, *Proper Confidence*, (London: SPCK, 1995), p 43.
2. Iris Murdoch, *Metaphysics as a Guide to Morals*, (London: Chatto & Windus, 1992), p 8.
3. See especially: Peter S. Hawkins, *The Language of Grace: Flannery O'Connor, Walker Percy & Iris Murdoch*, (Cambridge MA: Cowley Publications, 1981), and Rowan Williams, *Lost Icons*, (London and New York: Continuum, 2000).
4. See Suzanne Langer, *Philospophy in a New Key*, (Harvard University Press, 1942).
5. Iris Murdoch, 'On 'God' and 'Good'', in *Existentialists and Mystics*, (London: Chatto and Windus, 1997) p 344.
6. Murdoch, *Metaphysics as a Guide to Morals*, p 59.


CHAPTER 8

1. Albert Nolan, quoted by Angela Hanley, 'Women and Men Doing Theology Together', *Spirituality*, Vol 12, No 64, January-February 2006, pp 24-8, pp 25-6.
2. Angela Hanley, *Spirituality*, pp 24-8, p 26.
3. Stephen R. White, *A Space for Belief*, (Dublin: Columba Press, 2006, see especially Introduction and Chapter 1.
4. Oliver Davies, *A Theology of Compassion*, (London, SCM Press, 2001), p 260.
5. Marcus Braybrooke, *Explorer's Guide to Christianity*, (London: Hodder & Stoughton, 1998), p xv.

6. Stanley Hauerwas, *With the Grain of the Universe*, (London: SCM Press, 2002), p 10. 'Any theology that threatens to become a position more determinative than the Christian practice of prayer betrays its subject. At best, theology is but a series of reminders to help Christians pray faithfully.'

7. Jürgen Moltmann, *The Crucified God*, (London: SCM Press, 1974 & 2001)

8. J. Denny Weaver, *The Non-Violent Atonement*, (Grand Rapids, MI: Eerdmans, 2001)

9. Braybrooke, p 116.

10. Braybrooke, p 10.

## CHAPTER 9

1. Stephen R. White, *The Right True End of Love*, (Dublin: The Columba Press, 2005).

2. Peter S. Hawkins, *The Language of Grace: Flannery O'Connor, Walker Percy & Iris Murdoch,* (Cambridge MA: Cowley Publications, 1983), pp 7-8.

3. Marcus Braybrooke, *Explorer's Guide to Christianity*, (London: Hodder & Stoughton, 1998), p 62.

4. Nicky Cruz, *Run, Baby Run*, (Many editions, most recently London: Hodder and Stoughton, 2003).

5. St Augustine, *Confessions*, trs R. S. Pine-Coffin, (London: Penguin, 1961), p 59. (Book 3:4)

## CHAPTER 10

1. See Stephen R. White, *A Space for Belief*, (Dublin: Columba Press, 2006).

2. See Stephen R. White, *The Right True End of Love*, (Dublin: Columba Press, 2005).

# Glossary of Theological Terms

*Adiaphora:* A term much beloved of the Reformers, indicating those things on which a difference of opinion or interpretation is permissible.

*Anhypostatic:* A term not actually employed during the patristic era, but representing the view (which was expressed although ultimately found heretical) that the human nature of Christ has no concrete subsistence of its own.

*Apophatic/Cataphatic:* Broadly corresponding to the negative/ positive approaches to theology respectively. Positive theology looks at God in relation to the world and uses universal terms such as 'Good' and 'Being'. Negative theology insists that God is ultimately a mystery and beyond all of these terms.

*Docetic:* Holding that Jesus Christ was a purely divine being who only had the appearance of being human.

*Enhypostatic:* Conveying the idea that the Godhead, incarnate in Jesus Christ, included all the attributes of human nature as perfected, and that therefore the one person of Christ, though divine, is fully human.

*Eschatology:* That part of Christian theology which is concerned with the final things, traditionally death, judgement, heaven and hell.

*Hermeneutical:* Concerning the principles which underlie the interpretation of scripture, especially with regard to how it applies in the here and now.

*Hypostatic:* The hypostatic union is the doctrine of the uhnion of divine and human natures in Jesus Christ without any confusion of their substances.

*Kenotic:* Referring to the laying aside of divine attributes by Christ, or his emptying himself of these attributes.

*Pericope:* A unit of biblical text such as a parable, a story or an item of teaching.

*Persona:* The Latin equivalent of Proposon – also originally meaning an actor's mask.

*Prosopon:* A Greek term originally meaning an actor's role or mask, but used theologically to mean the 'faces' of God – the persons of the Trinity.

*Telos:* The 'end' or purpose of something: the goal to which it tends.

# Index of Names